# kids' baking

hamlyn

# kids' baking

## 60 DELICIOUS RECIPES FOR CHILDREN TO MAKE

Sara Lewis

For Mitch, an enthusiastic and creative cake maker and taster.

First published in Great Britain in 2006
by Hamlyn, a division of Octopus Publishing Group Ltd
2-4 Heron Quays, London E14 4JP



Distributed in the United States and Canada by
Sterling Publishing Co., Inc.
387 Park Avenue South, New York, NY 10016-8810



ISBN-13: 978-0-600-61501-9
ISBN-10: 0-600-61501-4

A CIP catalogue record for this book is available from the British Library.

Printed and bound in China

10 9 8 7 6 5 4 3 2 1

## Notes

Standard level spoon measures are used in all recipes.

Ovens should be preheated to the specified temperature. If using a fan-assisted oven, follow the manufacturer's instructions for adjusting the time and temperature.

Medium eggs have been used throughout.

A few recipes include nuts and nut derivatives. Anyone with a known nut allergy must avoid these. Children under the age of 3 with a family history of nut allergy, asthma, eczema, or any type of allergy are also advised to avoid eating dishes which contain nuts. Do not give whole nuts or seeds to any child under 5 because of the risk of choking.

## Key

The apron symbol indicates recipes that are suitable for young or new cooks.

# contents

# baking with kids

What better way to relax with your child than to share the joy of making and baking cakes, cookies, or bread. The smell alone is wonderful as it drifts through the house and the compliments your child will reap will make them burst with pride, whether they are a young preschooler or a teenager with attitude. There are recipes for all ages and abilities—from easy all-in-one cakes ideal for the very young cook, and quick cakes to make after school, to something a little more ambitious for the older cook, such as some of the special cakes in the "Cakes to impress" chapter.

Cooking isn't just fun, it's educational, too, without your children even noticing it! Weighing out ingredients helps with basic arithmetic—from simple addition to fractions, not to mention the all-important skills of accuracy and attention to detail. In addition, mixing, spreading, and spooning all help with coordination. As your child grows in confidence and experience, parental input can become less and less, thereby increasing your child's independence and self-esteem.

For those children who are very fussy eaters, cooking can also encourage them to be more adventurous, to try foods as they prepare them and to inspire a love of food rather than the dread of stressful mealtime battles.

With more and more supermarkets stocking greater numbers of ready meals, we are in danger of bringing up a generation of children who can't or don't want to cook, preferring to sit in front of the TV or computer instead. Cooking at school is no longer an option for many children so it is up to us as parents or grandparents to encourage our children to want to learn. Luckily for me, I had a mom who let me take over the kitchen with my friend on a Saturday afternoon. We made a terrible mess and had a few disasters but always enjoyed tasting the end results. My own children love to cook—my daughter Alice keeps making muffins to soothe her exam nerves while my young son William is a griddle cake and chocolate spread fan.

Unlike many other activities you may do with your children, you don't need to travel, queue up, pay for classes, or buy lots of specialized equipment to enjoy cooking at home. The chances are you will have most of the ingredients in the pantry and you can eat the end result. So get baking together and have fun!

Sara Lewis

# kids in the kitchen

Baking is great fun for everyone but if you're planning to cook by yourself, always check with an adult before you begin. Make sure that you have all the necessary ingredients and all the right equipment, especially the right size cake pan (see page 12), before you start.

## getting started

First choose a recipe you would like to bake and make sure that you have the time to prepare and cook it—this is especially important if you are going out later. Collect together all the ingredients and equipment you will need. Turn on the oven so that it can be heating up ready for cooking, then begin measuring and weighing out your ingredients and away you go!

## hygiene and safety

Don't forget the following basic hygiene and safety rules when working in the kitchen:

- Always wash your hands before you begin.
- Tie back long hair.
- Wear an apron or old shirt to keep your clothes clean.
- Only use food that is within its "use-by" date and throw away any food that has been dropped on the floor.
- Make sure you have an adult with you when using sharp knives, electrical equipment, or the stove.
- Enjoy yourself cooking but don't play about in the kitchen or you could hurt yourself, as well as spoiling the recipe.

- If you're not sure what size saucepan to use, then choose a bigger one so that its contents will be less likely to boil over. Turn saucepan handles to the side of the stove, to avoid them being knocked as you pass by.
- Wipe up spilled food or liquids on the floor at once to avoid slipping on a greasy patch.
- Always use a pot holder when taking hot dishes out of the oven.
- Avoid damaging the countertop with sharp knives or hot dishes—always chop or cut food on a cutting board and put hot baking pans or saucepans on a heatproof mat, a wooden cutting board, or even the stove as long as nothing is cooking on it.

## cleaning up!

The tidying up afterward is not as much fun as cooking but it has to be done! Make sure you put away all unused ingredients, wash up and dry all the equipment you have used and wipe all the countertops with a clean damp cloth before you leave the kitchen. Then hang up any wet dishtowels to dry.

Don't forget to sweep the floor, too, as there are sure to be some floury and sticky bits, and remember to turn off the oven when you have finished with it.

## cooking with very little children

Young children need supervision in the kitchen at all times. Stand your child on a sturdy chair so that he or she can reach the countertop or sink. Alternatively, cover the floor with a plastic or PVC tablecloth then get the child to measure and mix while sitting on the cloth.

Some little children hate the feel of PVC aprons. If you don't have a cotton one that's small enough then use an old shirt of an older brother or sister as a cover up. Remember to allow plenty of time for your cooking as children hate to be hurried.

When the cooking's done, it's good practice to involve little ones in the cleaning up, too. Even tiny children can have a go at washing up if you give them plenty of time and encouragement and keep the mop handy for sorting out any spills.

# kitchen equipment

The required equipment (and ingredients) are listed in order of use throughout the recipes in this book. Most of the equipment needed for baking will be things you already have at home. Microwaves and electric mixers have been given as options to help save time and effort but are not essential.

## measuring

Accurate measuring is very important when you cook. If you don't measure out your ingredients carefully the recipes won't work! Before you get started baking, make sure you have each of the following items to hand:

### measuring cups and spoons

If you don't already have a set of plastic or metal measuring cups and spoons then these are a must. Fill with the ingredient then level the top with the back of a knife. Don't be tempted to use a rounded measure as this may give you almost double the amount of ingredient that the recipe actually needs. Everyday cutlery should not be used for measuring as the designs, depths, and shapes of the spoons vary so much.

### measuring jugs

Use either a plastic or a heavy-duty glass jug. Fill it to the required level then double-check the quantity by setting the jug on a hard surface so that the contents are level.

### scales

Digital add-and-weigh scales are the easiest and clearest to use as the amount is shown as a number with pinpoint accuracy, whereas balance scales need a little more skill.

## mixing

Most homes will have at least one glass or plastic bowl suitable for mixing ingredients in. If you are short of bowls then use cereal bowls for small amounts or a large casserole dish for mixing.

Always use a wooden spoon to stir ingredients being heated in a saucepan as metal spoons become too hot to hold and will also damage the surface of a nonstick saucepan.

## using a microwave

Microwaves are great for saving time, especially when softening butter or melting chocolate. Always use china, plastic, or heavy glass bowls in the microwave. Don't use metal containers or dishes with silver or gold decoration as these will make sparks when the microwave is turned on.

## using an electric mixer

A hand-held electric beater is probably the easiest electrical gadget worth having in the kitchen. It saves a lot of time, especially when creaming butter and sugar together, beating egg whites, or whipping cream.

Carefully fix the two metal beaters in place before you switch on the beater or they may fall out in the middle of mixing. Do turn off the electricity before you take them out to wash.

If you use a food processor instead, then fit it with the plastic blade before use. The powerful motor makes light work of mixing cakes and, unlike with a hand-held mixer, any flour that may fly up during mixing is kept in the bowl beneath the tight-fitting lid. If adding fruit to the mixture then mix it very briefly for just a matter of seconds or the fruit will be very finely chopped and lose all definition in the cake.

**OVEN KNOW-HOW**

- Although all ovens are supposed to run at a certain temperature, many run slightly hotter or colder so check with a parent before you begin cooking. Fan-assisted ovens always run hotter so reduce the temperature or cooking time slightly, according to the manufacturer's instructions.
- Cook cakes on the center oven shelf.
- Check on the cake's progress toward the end of cooking time and if it looks done, even though there is still time to run, then test it (see page 18). If it still needs longer but you feel it might overbrown, then cover the top loosely with a piece of foil and put back in the oven.
- When making a large cake don't be tempted to open the oven door until at least halfway through the cooking time, or the cake will sink because of the rush of cold air that hits it.

# cake pans

You will see from the recipes that you can use all sorts of pans in which to make cakes—from roasting pans and tart pans to the more traditional cake pans. For baking cookies and some breads, you need only one or two good-quality baking sheets.

## choosing your pan

The number of different cake pans listed in the box opposite seems high, but remember that there are 60 recipes in this book, which is a lot of different cakes, cookies, and loaves!

If you don't have the right size of pan improvise with what you do have, but check on the cake's progress in the oven. The larger the pan, the thinner the cake will be and the less cooking time it will require.

If you want to use a square pan instead of a round one then go down a size. For example, if the recipe calls for an 8 inch round pan, then the cake mixture will also fit into a 7 inch square pan.

## lining cake pans

Unless you use cake pans with a nonstick surface it is usually best to line at least the base of the pan with a piece of lining paper.

You can use nonstick parchment paper or waxed paper to line cake pans. The difference is that nonstick parchment paper has been specially treated and does not need to be brushed with oil to stop food sticking to it, whereas waxed paper needs a light brushing with cooking oil.

**USEFUL BAKING PANS**

- 2 nonstick baking sheets
- 7 inch round deep cake pan
- 7 inch round, removable-bottomed, deep cake pan
- two 8 inch layer cake pans
- 8 inch round springform pan or removable-bottomed pan
- 8 inch fluted-edged, removable-bottomed tart pan
- 11 inch fluted-edged, removable-bottomed tart pan
- 7 inch square deep cake pan
- 8 inch square deep cake pan
- 8 inch square shallow cake pan
- 12-hole deep muffin pan
- 12-hole muffin pan
- 2 lb loaf pan with a base measurement of 7½ x 3½ inches and 3 inches deep
- small roasting pan with a base measurement of 7 x 11 inches and about 1½ inches deep
- medium roasting pan with a base measurement of 12 x 9 inches and about 1½ inches deep

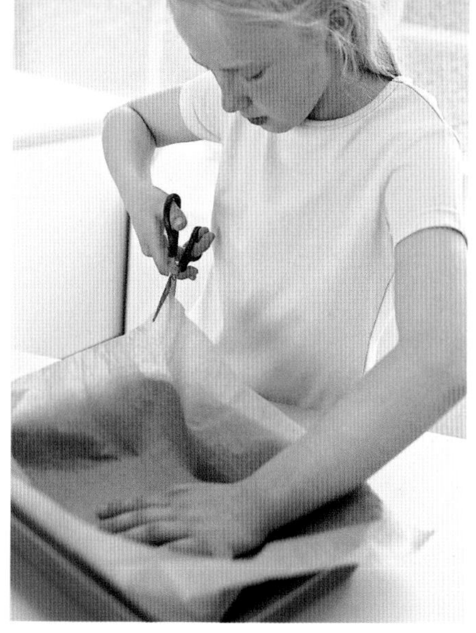

## baking sheets

Brush baking sheets with a little cooking oil before use.

## layer cake pans

Brush the base and sides of the pans with a little oil then stand one of the pans on a double thickness piece of waxed paper. Draw around the pan, cut out the shape, then press a paper circle on to the base of each pan and brush the paper lightly with a little extra oil.

## deep round or square pans

Deep pans can be base-lined in the same way as a layer cake pan or the sides may need lining, too, if the cake takes a long time to cook—see each recipe for details.

If lining the base and sides of the pan, first stand the pan on a piece of nonstick parchment paper, rather than waxed paper. Draw around the pan then cut out the shape for the base. Next cut a strip of paper, a little higher than the cake pan sides and long enough to go all the way round the cake pan and overlap slightly. Fold up the bottom edge by about ½ inch then make small scissor cuts up to the fold line at intervals along the strip of paper for a round pan, or just at the corners for a square or rectangular-shaped pan. Arrange the paper strip around the inside of the pan so that the folded and snipped edge is at the bottom of the pan and the ends of the long strip overlap slightly. Place the paper base on top.

## roasting pans

Cut a large piece of nonstick parchment paper a little larger than the pan, make diagonal cuts into the corners of the paper then press into the pan, tucking the snipped edges one behind the other for a snug fit over the base and up the sides of the pan.

## loaf pans

Brush the inside of the pan with a little oil then cut a strip of waxed paper the length of the longest side and wide enough to go over the base and up the two long sides of the pan. Press the paper into the pan and brush with a little extra oil.

Alternatively, line the loaf pan with a large piece of nonstick parchment paper, snip into the corners of the paper as if lining a roasting pan then press into the pan (there is no need to oil the pan or the paper).

# cake-making techniques

Cake-making really is not difficult. There are various different ways to make cakes. Once you get to know these basic techniques you should enjoy success every time and be able to impress your friends and family with your baking skills and tasty results!

## rubbing in

This method is most often used for making scones, shortbread cookies, and loaf cakes.

- Put the flour and sugar in a large bowl then cut the butter into small pieces and add to the bowl.
- Lift a little of the butter and flour out of the bowl and, with the palms of your hands facing upward, rub the flour and fat across your fingers with your thumbs.
- Try to use butter or margarine that is at room temperature so that it will be easier for you to rub into pieces. If it is very hard when you take it out of the refrigerator, then soften (but don't melt) it for a few seconds in the microwave before you cut it into pieces.
- If you have a hand-held electric mixer or a food processor, you may like to use this instead of your fingertips.
- Stir in the required flavorings then mix with beaten eggs, milk, or fruit juices, or for shortbread simply squeeze the crumbs together to make a dough.

## melting

With this method, the cake is made by melting together butter with sugar, light corn syrup, honey, or molasses, and then mixing this with dry ingredients such as flour, spices, nuts, seeds, oats, and granola.

- Use a medium or large saucepan so that there will be plenty of room to mix in the next ingredients.
- Stir the mixture while melting to make sure that all the butter has melted and the sugar has completely dissolved.
- Keep the heat low so that the mixture does not burn.
- Take the pan off the heat and mix in the dry ingredients.

## creaming

This method involves creaming or beating together the fat and sugar and is most often used for large special cakes.

- First beat the butter (kept at room temperature, so that it is soft) or soft margarine and sugar together in a mixing bowl until light and fluffy, using either a wooden spoon or an electric beater.
- Gradually mix in alternate spoonfuls of beaten egg and flour until the mixture is smooth. Do not add the eggs all at once or the mixture will separate or "curdle."

## using eggs

Eggs are widely used in baking, either whole or separated into yolks and whites.

- To break open an egg, crack the shell by tapping its center over the rim of the bowl.
- Hold the egg over the bowl, enlarge the crack with your fingers until the egg is almost in two halves.
- Tip the egg into the bowl and beat it with a fork until an even yellow. Discard the shell.

### separating an egg

- Crack the egg as above but as you enlarge the crack and separate the shell, try to keep the yolk in one of the halves so that the white runs between the shells into the bowl.
- Gently tip the egg yolk into the other half shell so that any remaining egg white caught by the first shell half drops into the bowl, then tip the yolk into another bowl.
- If you drop a little egg yolk into the bowl of egg whites, don't worry, just scoop it out with a jagged piece of egg shell.

## single-stage, or all-in-one cakes

This type of cake is perhaps the easiest of all cakes to make as all the ingredients are put into the bowl at the same time and mixed together.

Single-stage cakes are usually made with soft margarine, but butter that has been stored at room temperature or softened in the microwave for a few seconds can also be used. They often include a little baking powder as well as self-rising flour to make sure that they rise well.

## whipping egg whites

- The secret to whipping egg whites is to use a bowl that is completely dry and clean, the whisk or beaters must also be clean and dry and there must be no egg yolk present. Any traces of butter or margarine will also stop the egg whites from whipping up.
- A hand-held electric beater will beat eggs quickly, but if you don't have one then use a balloon whisk or rotary beater and try to get a brother, sister, or parent to share the work.
- As you use the beater, you will see the clear egg whites turn to a frothy foam. As more air is trapped, it will become a thick white mixture that can be lifted into peaks.
- To check whether the egg whites are thick enough, tilt the bowl. If they slide, then beat a little longer until you feel brave enough to turn the bowl upside down without them falling out!
- The egg whites can hold the trapped air for only a short while, so use them quickly before they have a chance to deflate.

## using yeast

All the recipes in the bread chapter use active dry yeast. Simply stir it into the flour, adding salt for flavor and a little sugar as food for the yeast, then activate the yeast with warm water or milk. Warmth is the key, so make sure that the water is warm enough to encourage the yeast to grow and multiply but not so hot that it kills it or so cold that it won't get the yeast started.

If you are not sure what kind of yeast you have then read the back of the package carefully.

# baking tips

Once your cake, cookies, or bread are in the oven, you can start cleaning up the kitchen, but don't forget your creation and leave it in the oven to burn! Unless the cake is to be served warm, like scones or muffins, let it cool completely before serving or storing it in an airtight container.

## is my cake or bread cooked?

Always take great care when testing cakes, cookies, and bread as they will be hot and the pans could easily burn your hands. Always use pot holders and make sure an adult is there to help you if necessary.

### cupcakes and layer cakes (1)

Press the top of the cake lightly with a fingertip—if the cake springs back it is ready. If a dent remains then put the cake back in the oven and check again at 5-minute intervals.

### cookies

When cooked, cookies should be golden brown on top and still slightly soft underneath—they will harden on cooling.

### large cakes (2)

Push a fine metal skewer or wooden toothpick into the center of the cake and bring it out. If the skewer looks clean and dry, the cake is ready; if it is messy and sticky with cake mixture, the cake is not cooked through. Put it back in the oven and check again at 10- to 15-minute intervals.

1

2

3

### breads (3)

Tap the top or bottom with your fingertips—if it sounds hollow then it is ready. If you are unsure when making a large loaf then tap on the top, loosen and remove it from the pan then tap the base to double-check. If the base seems a little soft and damp then put the bread back in the oven without the pan, straight onto the oven shelf, and test again after 5 minutes.

## what went wrong?

Sometimes things go wrong in cake-making. Don't be disheartened—just look at the suggestions below as to where you might have gone wrong, work out the problem and try the recipe again.

### if the cake sank...

- Perhaps you kept opening the oven door during cooking.
- Did you take the cake out of the oven before it was fully cooked?
- Did you forget to use one of the ingredients?
- Perhaps you used too much baking powder. Did you use an accurate spoon measure, or an ordinary spoon from the cutlery drawer?

### if the cake has not risen...

- The oven may have been at too low a temperature, or turned off accidentally.
- Perhaps you did not use enough baking powder or soda.
- You may have used all-purpose flour instead of self-rising.
- Perhaps the whipped-in air was knocked out when folding in egg whites (as for a cheesecake) or flour (as for a jelly roll).

**STORAGE**

**Once your cake or cookies have completely cooled put them in an airtight container and store in a cool place. For large cakes it can be helpful to put the cake on the lid then cover with the upside-down container so that it is easier to slice the cake while still in the container. Keep cakes with cream or cream cheese fillings or frosting in the refrigerator.**

### if the cake has cracked and is too brown on top...

- The oven was probably too hot. (If using a fan-assisted oven, was the necessary adjustment made to the temperature?)
- The cake may have been cooked on too high an oven shelf.

### if the fruit in the cake has sunk to the bottom...

- There may have been too much liquid in the cake. If large eggs were used instead of medium ones, the cake mixture may have been too wet to hold the fruit up.

# cook's terms

## baking
To cook food in the oven.

## beating
To soften an ingredient or mix it with another ingredient, usually using a wooden spoon or a fork.

## chopping (1)
To cut food into tiny pieces.

## chunks
Pieces of food in larger pieces than diced food (*see* "dicing").

## creaming
To beat butter or margarine together with sugar using a wooden spoon or an electric mixer until light and fluffy and very smooth.

## decorating
To finish off the top of a cake or cookies attractively.

## dicing
To cut food into small cubes about the size of your fingernail.

## draining
To pour off the liquid from food through a strainer or colander.

## drizzling
To spoon wiggly scribble-like lines of icing or melted chocolate over the top of a baked cake or cookies, or to sprinkle a little oil over bread dough before baking.

## folding in (2)
To mix ingredients together with a very gentle stirring action to keep the air in the mixture, for example when mixing in whipped cream for a filling, when folding in flour to a jelly roll mixture or when folding beaten egg whites into a cheesecake mixture.

- Use a metal spoon such as a dessertspoon or serving spoon with a large bowl and gently stir the spoon through the two different mixtures in a figure of eight or swirling movement.
- Slowly turn the spoon so that the mixture on the bottom of the bowl is gently lifted and mixed with that on the top.

## grating
To make tiny pieces, by rubbing an ingredient such as an orange, lemon, lime, or block of cheese against a grater—a metal blade with small rough-edged holes pressed into it.

## greasing (3)
To coat a cooking utensil such as a cake pan with a little cooking oil or softened butter or margarine, to prevent food sticking when cooked.

1

2

3

## kneading (4)

To smooth the outside of a dough when making shortbread cookies, scones, pastry, and bread.

- Sprinkle a little flour onto the countertop then tip the dough out on top. Fold half of the dough back on itself using your hands, then turn slightly and do this a few more times until the dough is smooth.
- Unlike shortbread or scones, bread that has yeast added needs a lot of kneading and can take quite rough treatment. Clench your fist and press into the dough to stretch it, then fold the dough back, turn it and repeat for 5 minutes. This will seem like ages, so check with the clock so that you know what time you started. After a few minutes you will begin to feel and see the difference and the more you knead, the less flour you will need on the countertop to stop the dough sticking.

## lining (5)

To put waxed or nonstick parchment paper into the base or the base and sides of a cake pan so that the cake does not stick to the pan when cooked (see page 12).

## sieving

Another term for sifting ingredients (*see* "sifting").

## sifting

To remove the lumps from dry ingredients such as flour, cocoa powder, brown sugar, and confectioners' sugar by pressing or shaking them through the fine mesh of a sifter.

- Rest the handle and edges of the sifter over a mixing bowl.
- Add the ingredient to be sifted then press it through the holes of the sifter using the back of a metal spoon.

## simmering

To cook liquid in a saucepan over a gentle heat so that bubbles just break the surface.

## squeezing (6)

To press the juice from a lemon, lime, or orange, using a lemon squeezer.

## whipping

To beat air into ingredients such as egg whites, whole eggs and sugar, or cream using a balloon whisk, rotary or electric beaters so that they become very thick.

## whisking

Another term for whipping (*see* "whipping").

4

5

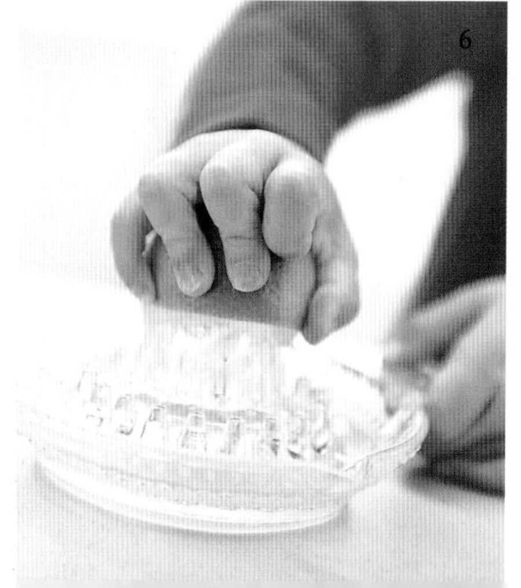
6

# double berry muffins

makes 12

## equipment

12 paper bake cups

12-hole deep muffin pan

measuring cups and spoons

large mixing bowl

fork

small saucepan or microwave-proof bowl

2 dessertspoons

dull knife

wire rack

## ingredients

2½ cups all-purpose flour

3 teaspoons baking powder

½ cup superfine sugar

¼ cup butter

3 eggs

⅔ cup plain yogurt

4 tablespoons sunflower oil

1½ teaspoons vanilla extract

½ cup fresh blueberries

½ cup fresh raspberries

4

## what to do

**1**
- Set the oven to 400°F.
- Separate the paper bake cups and put one in each hole in the muffin pan.

**2**
- Put the flour, baking powder, and sugar in the mixing bowl and stir together using the fork.

**3**
- Melt the butter in the saucepan on the burner, or in the bowl in the microwave on full power for 30 seconds.
- Pour the melted butter into the flour and sugar mixture.

4

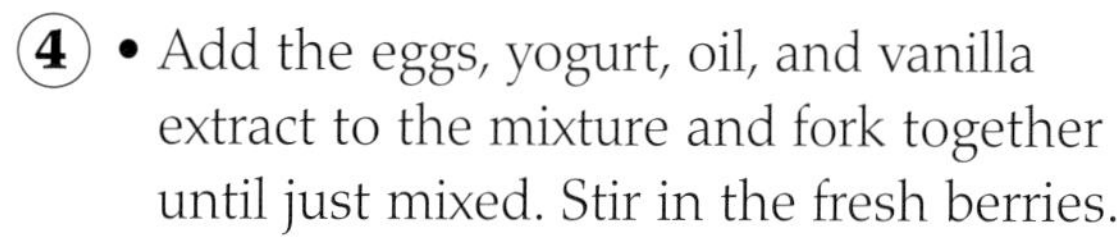

**4** • Add the eggs, yogurt, oil, and vanilla extract to the mixture and fork together until just mixed. Stir in the fresh berries.

**5** • Divide the mixture between the paper bake cups using 2 spoons.

• Bake for 15 minutes until the muffins are well risen and the tops have cracked and turned golden brown. Loosen the edges of the paper cups with the dull knife then transfer to the wire rack. Serve the muffins warm—they are best eaten on the day they are made.

# banana and poppy seed muffins

## equipment

12 paper bake cups

12-hole deep muffin pan

measuring cups and spoons

large mixing bowl

small saucepan or microwave-proof bowl

plate

fork

dessertspoon

dull knife

wire rack

## ingredients

2 cups self-rising flour

½ cup superfine sugar

2 tablespoons poppy seeds (optional)

¼ cup butter

1 ripe banana, about 5 oz before peeling

2 eggs

4 tablespoons plain yogurt

## what to do

**1** • Set the oven to 400°F.

• Separate the paper bake cups and put one in each hole in the muffin pan.

**2** • Put the flour, sugar, and poppy seeds, if using, in the mixing bowl.

**3** • Melt the butter in the saucepan on the burner, or in the bowl in the microwave on full power for 30 seconds.

• Peel then mash the banana on the plate using the fork.

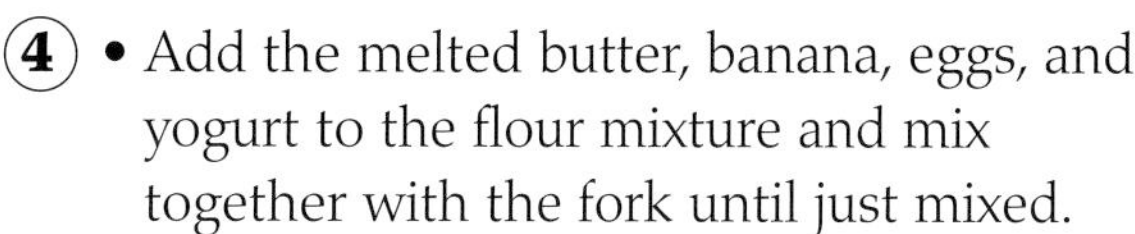

**4** • Add the melted butter, banana, eggs, and yogurt to the flour mixture and mix together with the fork until just mixed.

**5** • Spoon the muffin mixture into the paper bake cups. Bake for 15 minutes until the muffins are well risen and golden brown.

• Loosen the edges of the paper cups with the dull knife then transfer them to the wire rack to cool. Serve the muffins warm or cold—they are best eaten on the day they are made.

# christmas muffins

makes 12

## equipment

12 foil or paper bake cups

12-hole muffin pan

kitchen scale, measuring cups, spoons, and jug

large mixing bowl

wooden spoon

small saucepan or microwave-proof bowl

fork

dessertspoon

dull knife

wire rack

rolling pin

2½ inch round and star-shaped cookie cutter

## ingredients

2½ cups all-purpose flour

3 teaspoons baking powder

1 teaspoon ground cinnamon

½ teaspoon ground ginger

½ cup dark brown sugar

1⅓ cups mixed dried fruit

⅓ cup butter

3 eggs

⅔ cup milk

*To finish*

3 tablespoons apricot jelly

confectioners' sugar, for dusting the countertop

8 oz marzipan or ready-to-roll white fondant icing dough

red, yellow, and green icing decorator tubes

## what to do

**1**
- Set the oven to 400°F.
- Separate the bake cups and put one in each hole in the muffin pan.

**2**
- Put the flour, baking powder, spices, sugar, and dried fruit in the mixing bowl and stir together.
- Melt the butter in the saucepan on the burner, or in the bowl in the microwave on full power for 1 minute.
- Mix the melted butter, eggs, and milk together with the fork then add to the flour mixture and stir until just mixed.

4

4

3 • Spoon the mixture into the bake cups. Bake for 15 minutes until the muffins are well risen and browned.

• Loosen the edges of the cups from the pan with the dull knife then transfer to the wire rack.

4 • To decorate the muffins, spread a little jelly over the top of each muffin.

• Sprinkle the countertop with a little confectioners' sugar then knead the marzipan or ready-to-roll fondant and roll out thinly.

• Stamp out circles or stars using the cookie cutter and press one on the top of each muffin. Reknead and roll out the trimmings and continue until all the muffins have been topped.

5 • Decorate the top of each cake with colored icing. Leave the icing to harden before serving the muffins—they are best eaten on the day they are made.

## tip

★ If you are short of time then serve the muffins without the decoration.

# cheesy corn muffins

## equipment

- 12 paper bake cups
- 12-hole muffin pan
- kitchen scale, measuring cups, spoons, and jug
- grater
- plate
- large mixing bowl
- dessertspoon
- fork
- dull knife
- wire rack

## ingredients

- 4 oz mature cheddar cheese
- 3/4 cup quick-cook cornmeal
- 1 1/2 cups self-rising flour
- 2 teaspoons baking powder
- 2/3 cup milk
- 2 eggs
- 2 teaspoons Dijon mustard
- 4 tablespoons sunflower oil
- salt and pepper
- butter, to serve

## what to do

**1**
- Set the oven to 400°F.
- Separate the paper bake cups and put one in each hole in the muffin pan.
- Coarsely grate the cheese onto the plate.

**2**
- Put the cornmeal, flour, and baking powder in the mixing bowl. Stir in the cheese.
- Put the milk, eggs, mustard, and oil in the measuring jug and add a little salt and pepper. Beat together using the fork.
- Add the milk mixture to the cornmeal mixture and stir until just mixed.

3 • Spoon the muffin mixture into the paper bake cups. Bake for 15 minutes until the muffins are well risen and golden brown.

• Loosen the edges of the paper cups with the dull knife then transfer to the wire rack. Serve the muffins warm, broken, and spread with butter—they are best eaten on the day they are made.

## tip

★ If you don't have any cornmeal replace it with the same quantity of all-purpose flour.

# apricot and white chocolate rockies

makes 24

## equipment

pastry brush
2 baking sheets
kitchen scale, measuring cups, and spoons
scissors
plastic bag
rolling pin
medium mixing bowl
dull knife
plate
electric mixer (optional)
dessertspoon
teaspoon
spatula
wire rack

## ingredients

oil, for greasing
⅔ cup ready-to-eat dried apricots
4 oz white chocolate
2 cups self-rising flour
½ cup butter, at room temperature
⅓ cup superfine sugar
1 egg
2–3 tablespoons milk

## what to do

1
- Set the oven to 350°F.
- Lightly brush the baking sheets with a little oil.
- Snip the apricots into small pieces with the scissors.
- Put the chocolate in the plastic bag. Break it into pieces with the rolling pin.

1

3

2 • Put the flour in the mixing bowl. Cut the butter into pieces on the plate then add to the flour. Rub the butter into the flour between your fingertips to make tiny crumbs, or use an electric mixer.

• Stir in the sugar, snipped apricots, and broken chocolate.

• Add the egg then mix in enough milk to make a soft lumpy-looking mixture.

3 • Using the dessertspoon and teaspoon, scoop and drop 24 mounds of the mixture onto the greased baking sheets, leaving a little space in between to allow them to spread during cooking.

• Bake for 12–15 minutes until the cookies are pale golden and just firm to the touch.

• Loosen the cookies with the spatula then transfer to the wire rack to cool. Eat the cookies on the day they are made.

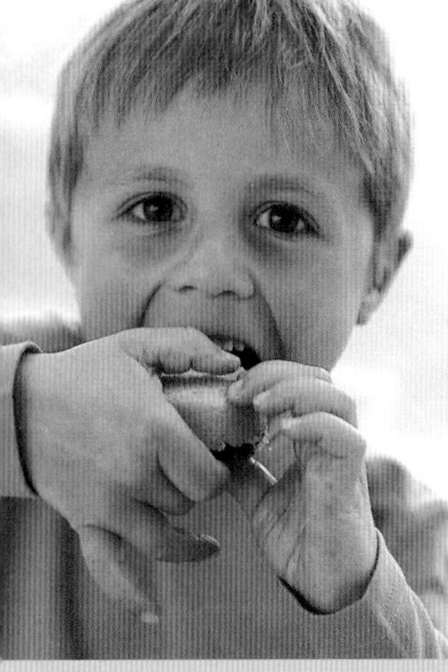

# mini raspberry sandwich cakes

makes 12

## equipment

pastry brush
12-hole deep muffin pan
scissors
waxed paper
measuring cups and spoons
large mixing bowl
wooden spoon or electric mixer
2 dessertspoons
teaspoon
dull knife
wire rack
sharp knife
sifter (optional)

## ingredients

oil, for greasing
¾ cup soft margarine
¾ cup superfine sugar
1½ cups self-rising flour
3 eggs

*To finish*

4 tablespoons seedless raspberry jelly
some fresh raspberries, to decorate
2 tablespoons superfine sugar or sifted confectioners' sugar

## what to do

**1**
- Set the oven to 350°F.
- Lightly brush the holes in the muffin pan with a little oil, line the bases with small circles of waxed paper and brush these lightly with a little extra oil.

**(2)**
- Put all the cake ingredients into the large mixing bowl and beat together with the wooden spoon or the electric mixer until smooth.

- Spoon the cake mixture into the holes in the muffin pan and smooth flat with the back of the teaspoon.

**3**
- Bake for 10–12 minutes until the cakes are well risen and golden, and the tops spring back when lightly pressed with a fingertip.
- Loosen the sides of the cakes with the dull knife then transfer to the wire rack and let cool.

**4**
- Cut each cake in half then spread the lower halves with the jelly. Replace the cake tops, add the raspberries and sprinkle with a little sugar. These cakes are best eaten on the day they are made.

# apple scones

## equipment

pastry brush

large baking sheet

small sharp knife

cutting board

vegetable peeler

measuring cups, spoons, and jug

small saucepan

medium and small bowls

dull knife

plate

electric mixer (optional)

large metal spoon

rolling pin

2 1/4 inch round cookie cutter

teaspoon

wire rack

## ingredients

oil, for greasing

1 dessert apple

1/3 cup butter

3 cups self-rising flour, plus a little extra for dusting the countertop

1 teaspoon ground cinnamon

1/3 cup superfine sugar

1 egg, beaten

2/3 cup milk, plus 2 tablespoons for glazing

*To serve*

blackberry jelly

whipped or clotted cream

3

## what to do

**1**
- Set the oven to 400°F.
- Brush the baking sheet with a little oil.

**2**
- Cut the apple into quarters, cut away the core then peel and dice.
- Heat 2 tablespoons of the butter in the saucepan, add the apple and cook gently, without a lid, for 5 minutes until softened.

**3**
- Put the flour, half the cinnamon and 4 tablespoons of sugar in the medium bowl.
- Cut the remaining butter into small pieces on the plate then add to the flour mixture. Rub the butter into the flour mixture between your fingertips to make tiny crumbs, or use an electric mixer.

- Add the cooked apples and the egg to the flour mixture then slowly stir in enough milk to mix to a soft dough.

4 • Sprinkle the countertop with flour, tip out the dough and knead lightly until smooth.

- Roll out until about 1 inch thick. Using the cookie cutter, stamp out as many circles as you can and place them on the oiled baking sheet.
- Shape the trimmings into a ball then roll out again and cut more circles. Keep doing this until all the dough has been used up.

5 • Brush the tops of the scones with milk.

- Mix the remaining sugar and cinnamon together in the small bowl then sprinkle over the tops of the scones.
- Bake for 12–15 minutes until the scones are well risen and browned. Remove from the baking sheet and transfer to the wire rack. Serve the scones warm, split and filled with blackberry jelly and whipped cream.

# butterfly cakes

makes 12

## equipment

12 paper bake cups

12-hole muffin pan

measuring cups and spoons

large and medium mixing bowls

wooden spoon or electric mixer

dessertspoon

teaspoon

small sharp knife

dull knife

cutting board

## ingredients

½ cup soft margarine

½ cup superfine sugar

1 cup self-rising flour

2 eggs

1 teaspoon vanilla extract

*Frosting*

⅓ cup butter, at room temperature

1¼ cups confectioners' sugar

½ teaspoon vanilla extract

1–2 teaspoons milk

*To finish*

sugar strands

tubes of different colored icing

selection of candies

strips of candied angelica

## what to do

**1**
- Set the oven to 350°F.
- Separate the paper bake cups and put one in each hole in the muffin pan.

**2**
- Put all the cake ingredients in the large mixing bowl and beat with the wooden spoon or electric mixer until smooth.
- Spoon the cake mixture into the cups.

**3**
- Bake for 15–18 minutes until the cakes are well risen and golden brown, and the tops spring back when lightly pressed.

5

5

- Allow the cakes to cool in the pan.

**4** • Meanwhile, make the frosting. Put the butter into the second bowl and gradually beat in the confectioners' sugar (there is no need to sift it first), vanilla extract, and milk to make a smooth soft frosting.

**(5)** • Cut out a small circle of cake, about 1 inch in diameter, from the center of each cake by pressing the tip of the teaspoon at a slight angle into the center of the cake and twisting in much the same way as when using a pair of compasses.

- Fill the holes with most of the frosting.

- Cut the small cake circles in half to make "butterfly wings," spread thinly with the remaining frosting and press some sugar strands on top. Carefully stick these "wings" onto the frosting on the tops of the cakes.
- Pipe on wing shapes with colored tubes of icing. Add candies to some wings.
- Cut strips of angelica for the butterfly antennae. Dot one end of each strip with frosting and sprinkle with sugar strands. Press the other end into the frosting. The cakes can be stored in an airtight container for up to 2 days.

# meringues with lemon curd cream

makes 16

## equipment

large baking sheet
nonstick parchment paper
large and medium mixing bowls
electric beater
measuring cups and spoons
teaspoon
dessertspoon
dull knife
12 paper bake cups

## ingredients

3 egg whites
3/4 cup superfine sugar
2/3 cup heavy cream
2 tablespoons lemon curd
sugar flowers, to decorate

## what to do

**1**
- Set the oven to 225°F.
- Line the baking sheet with the nonstick parchment paper.

**(2)**
- Put the egg whites in the large mixing bowl and beat using the electric beater until very stiff. To test whether they are ready, turn the bowl upside down—if the eggs look like they may slide out, beat for a few minutes more.
- Gradually beat in the sugar a teaspoonful at a time and continue beating for 1–2 minutes more, even when all the sugar has been added, so that the meringue is very thick and glossy.

(2)

(3)

3 • Drop heaping teaspoonfuls of the meringue on the prepared baking sheet.

• Bake the meringues for about 1 hour until they are firm and can be lifted easily off the paper. If they stick on the bottom, cook them for 15 minutes longer.

• Allow the meringues to cool on the paper.

4 • Using the cleaned electric beater, whip the cream in the medium bowl until it has just thickened and makes soft swirls. Take care not to overwhip or it will look like butter.

• Stir the lemon curd into the cream then use it to sandwich the meringues together in pairs. Arrange them in the paper bake cups and decorate with sugar flowers. The meringues are best eaten on the day they are made, but unfilled ones may be stored in an airtight container for up to 5 days.

## tip

★ If you don't like lemon curd then leave it out of the cream.

# ricotta griddle cakes

## ingredients

- 1½ cups self-rising flour
- ½ teaspoon baking powder
- 1 tablespoon superfine sugar
- 8 oz tub ricotta cheese
- 3 eggs
- ¾ cup milk
- 2 tablespoons sunflower oil
- butter and jelly, to serve

## equipment

- measuring cups, spoons, and jug
- large mixing bowl
- balloon whisk
- paper towel
- griddle or heavy nonstick skillet
- large spoon
- spatula
- clean dish towel

## what to do

(1)
- Put the flour, baking powder, and sugar in the mixing bowl.
- Add the ricotta, the eggs, and a little of the milk and beat together until smooth. Gradually beat in the remaining milk.

(2)
- Pour the oil onto a folded piece of paper towel then rub over the surface of the griddle or heavy nonstick skillet and heat the pan.
- Drop spoonfuls of the mixture onto the hot griddle or skillet and cook for 3–4 minutes until bubbles form on the top and the cakes are golden brown underneath.

2

## tip

★ If you have an Aga or Rayburn cooker then lift the lid on the simmering plate and leave to cool for 1 minute, then wipe with the oiled paper towel and cook the cakes in batches straight on the simmering plate.

- Loosen the cakes and turn them over using the spatula. Cook the second side for 1–2 minutes until golden and the cakes are cooked through.
- Remove the cakes with the spatula and keep them hot wrapped in a clean dish towel. Cook the remaining mixture, wiping the griddle or pan with the oiled paper towel between batches as needed.

**3** • Serve the cakes while still hot, spread with butter and jelly.

# noah's ark cookies

makes 20

## equipment

measuring cups
dull knife
plate
large mixing bowl
electric mixer (optional)
nonstick parchment paper
rolling pin
animal-shaped cookie cutters
spatula
baking sheets
wire rack

## ingredients

¾ cup butter, at room temperature
⅓ cup superfine sugar
2¼ cups all-purpose flour

*To finish*

different colored icing decorator tubes
mini sugar-coated chocolate candies

## what to do

**1**
- Set the oven to 350°F.
- Cut the butter into small pieces on the plate then put in the bowl with the sugar and flour.
- Rub the butter into the flour mixture between your fingertips to make tiny crumbs, or use an electric mixer.
- Using your hands squeeze the cookie crumbs together to make a dough. Knead lightly then cut in half.

**2**
- Place one of the pieces of cookie dough between 2 large sheets of nonstick parchment paper then roll out thinly.
- Peel off the top piece of paper and stamp out animal shapes using a selection of different cookie cutters, making 2 of each animal shape.

2

2

## tips

★ Rolling out cookie mixture can be tricky for small children, so rolling it between 2 sheets of nonstick parchment paper helps to stop it sticking and breaking apart.

★ For chocolate-flavored animals, use 1 tablespoon less flour, adding unsweetened cocoa powder in its place.

**3**
- Carefully lift the cookie animals with the spatula and place on the ungreased baking sheets.
- Add the cookie trimmings to the other half of the cookie dough and squeeze together back into a ball. Continue rolling and stamping out the mixture until it has all been shaped into animals.

**4**
- Bake the cookies for about 10 minutes until they are pale golden. Allow to cool on the baking sheets, or transfer to the wire rack if preferred.

**5**
- When the cookies are cold, let your imagination run riot as you add the animal markings, piping features with tubes of colored icing and adding candies for eyes.
- Set the cookies aside for 30 minutes for the icing to harden before serving. They can be stored in an airtight container for up to 2 days.

# shortbread spirals

## equipment

measuring cups and spoons

small mug

teaspoon

dull knife

plate

2 mixing bowls

electric mixer (optional)

rolling pin

nonstick parchment paper

large baking sheet

## ingredients

2 tablespoons unsweetened cocoa powder

1 tablespoon boiling water

1 cup butter, at room temperature

2½ cups all-purpose flour

½ cup superfine sugar

1 teaspoon vanilla extract

## what to do

**1**
- Set the oven to 325°F.
- Put the cocoa powder into the mug and mix with the boiling water until smooth.

**2**
- Cut the butter into small pieces on the plate then put it in a mixing bowl with the flour and sugar. Rub the butter into the flour mixture with your fingertips to make tiny crumbs, or use an electric mixer.

**3**
- Spoon half the cookie mixture into the second bowl, add the cocoa paste to one and the vanilla extract to the other.
- Squeeze the crumbs and cocoa paste together with your hands until the crumbs begin to stick together and form an evenly colored dough. Wash your hands and repeat with the remaining crumbs and the vanilla extract.

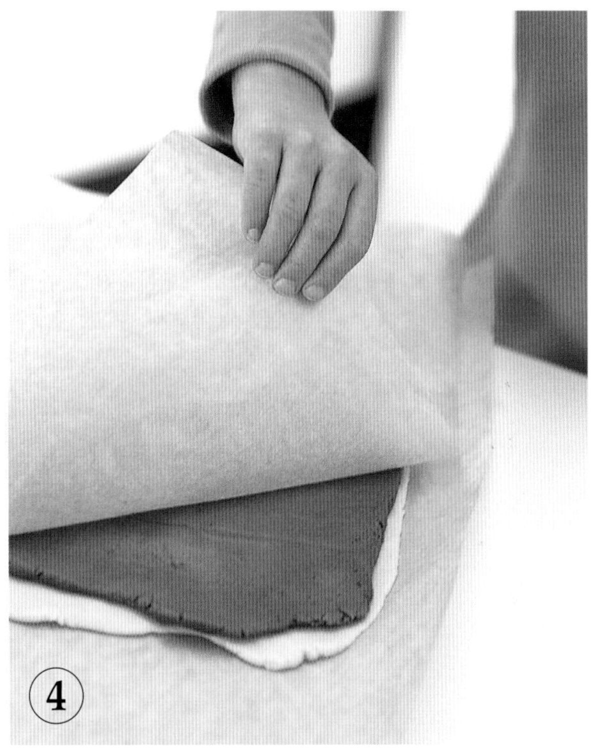

4 • Roll out the cocoa dough between 2 sheets of nonstick parchment paper to make an 8 inch square.

• Do the same with the vanilla dough, using another 2 sheets of nonstick parchment paper.

• Peel the top sheets off each piece of dough. Put the cocoa dough on top of the vanilla dough so that the base paper you were rolling out on is now on top. Peel this off then roll up the double cookie mixture into a long roll, peeling away the other sheet of paper as you go. Chill for 15 minutes.

5 • Cut the roll into 16 thick slices. Place on an ungreased baking sheet and cook for 8–10 minutes. Allow the cookies to cool on the baking sheet before serving.

# peanut butter cookies

makes 20

## equipment

pastry brush
2 baking sheets
measuring cups
plastic bag
rolling pin
large mixing bowl
wooden spoon or electric mixer
teaspoon
spatula
wire rack

## ingredients

oil, for greasing
½ cup unsalted peanuts
⅓ cup butter, at room temperature
⅓ cup superfine sugar
¼ cup light brown sugar
⅓ cup crunchy peanut butter
1¼ cups self-rising flour
1 egg

## what to do

1
- Set the oven to 350°F.
- Lightly brush the baking sheets with a little oil.
- Put the peanuts in the plastic bag and hit with the rolling pin until broken into chunky pieces.

2
- Put the butter and white and brown sugar in the bowl, add the peanut butter and beat together with the wooden spoon or electric mixer until soft and fluffy.

- Add the flour, egg, and two-thirds of the chopped nuts and stir together, squeezing with your hands when the mixture becomes too stiff to stir, until a soft dough is formed.

**3** • Shape teaspoonfuls of the cookie mixture into 20 balls with your hands. Place on the oiled baking sheets, leaving a little space in between to allow them to spread during cooking.

- Press the remaining nuts on top of the cookies, then bake for 10–12 minutes until the cookies are golden brown.

**4** • Allow to cool and harden on the baking sheets for 15 minutes then loosen with the spatula and transfer to the wire rack to cool completely.The cookies can be stored in an airtight container for up to 3 days.

# melting moments

## ingredients

oil, for greasing
½ cup butter
½ cup superfine sugar
1 egg
grated zest of ½ orange
1½ cups self-rising flour
½ cup rolled oats
6 candied cherries

makes 24

## equipment

pastry brush
2 baking sheets
measuring cups
large mixing bowl
wooden spoon or electric mixer
grater
plate
teaspoon
small sharp knife
cutting board
spatula
wire rack

## what to do

**1**
- Set the oven to 350°F.
- Lightly brush the baking sheets with a little oil.

**2**
- Put the butter and sugar in the mixing bowl and beat with the wooden spoon or electric mixer until light and fluffy.
- Add the egg and orange zest then the flour. Mix until smooth.

**3**
- Put the oats on the plate.
- Shape teaspoonfuls of the cookie mixture into 24 balls with your hands then roll the balls in the oats.
- Put the cookies on the oiled baking sheets, leaving a little space for them to spread during cooking. Quarter the cherries and press a piece into each cookie.

**4** • Bake the cookies for 12–15 minutes until they are lightly browned. Allow to cool and harden on the baking sheets for 15 minutes then transfer to the wire rack to cool completely. The cookies can be stored in an airtight container for up to 3 days.

# ruby fruit shorties

## ingredients

$^{2}/_{3}$ cup butter, at room temperature

$^{1}/_{3}$ cup light brown sugar

$^{1}/_{4}$ cup superfine sugar

1 egg

1 teaspoon vanilla extract

2 cups all-purpose flour

$^{1}/_{2}$ cup mixed dried blueberries and cherries

## equipment

measuring cups and spoons

large mixing bowl

wooden spoon or electric mixer

nonstick parchment paper, kitchen foil, or plastic wrap

dull knife

baking sheet

wire rack

## what to do

**1**
- Set the oven to 350°F.
- Put the butter, brown and white sugar in the bowl and beat with the wooden spoon or electric mixer until light and fluffy.

**2**
- Add the egg, vanilla extract, and flour and gently stir together until smooth.
- Mix in the dried fruits to make a smooth soft dough.
- Spoon the cookie mixture into a line along a piece of nonstick parchment paper, kitchen foil, or plastic wrap. Pat it into an even shape about 12 inches long. Wrap it up. Roll the cookie mixture backward and forward to neaten the shape. Chill for at least 15 minutes or up to 2 days.

3 • Unwrap and cut the mixture into 18 slices. Put them on an ungreased baking sheet and cook for 12–15 minutes until the cookies are a pale golden color.

4 • Allow the cookies to cool for a few minutes then loosen them with the knife. Transfer them to the wire rack to cool completely. The cookies can be stored in an airtight container for up to 3 days.

## tip

★ Instead of the berries use raisins, chopped dates, chopped dried apricots, chopped candied cherries, or a mixture of these, if you'd like.

# iced stars

## ingredients

2 egg whites

1½ cups confectioners' sugar

½ teaspoon ground cinnamon

1⅔ cups ground almonds

2–3 teaspoons fresh lemon juice

oil, for greasing

shiny colored balls

makes 25

## equipment

large and small mixing bowls

electric beater

measuring cups and spoons

teaspoon

tablespoon

plastic wrap

lemon squeezer

pastry brush

2 baking sheets

rolling pin

nonstick parchment paper

2½ inch star-shaped cookie cutter

dull knife

## what to do

**1**
- Put the egg whites into the large mixing bowl and beat using the electric beater until stiff and standing in peaks.
- Gradually beat in the sugar a teaspoonful at a time. Add the cinnamon and beat for 1–2 minutes more until the meringue is thick and glossy.

**2**
- Spoon 6 tablespoons of the meringue mixture into the smaller bowl, cover the bowl with plastic wrap and set aside for later.
- Add the ground almonds to the large bowl of meringue and gently fold together. Gradually fold in enough lemon juice to make a thick paste.
- Cover the bowl with plastic wrap and chill for 1 hour.
- Set the oven to 350°F.
- Lightly brush the baking sheets with a little oil.

3 • Roll out the almond dough between 2 large sheets of nonstick parchment paper until it is about ¼ inch thick.

• Peel off the top piece of paper and stamp stars out of the dough using the cookie cutter. Carefully transfer the star-shaped cookies to the oiled baking sheets. Shape the trimmings into a ball and roll out on the paper. Stamp out more stars until all the cookie mixture has been used.

**4** • Bake the cookies for about 5 minutes, changing the baking sheets over halfway through cooking, then remove the baking sheets from the oven and reduce the temperature to 225°F.

• Spoon a little of the reserved meringue on to each cookie then, using a pastry brush or the tip or a knife, ease the meringue all over the hot cookies.

• Press the shiny colored balls onto the star points. Return the cookies to the oven for 5 minutes until the meringue icing has dried out but not browned.

• Loosen the cookies with a spatula, then leave to cool. The cookies can be stored in an airtight container for up to 5 days.

makes 10

## equipment

measuring cups and spoons

1 large and 2 small mixing bowls

wooden spoon or electric mixer

sifter

teaspoon

2 large baking sheets

fork

dull knife

# chocolate kisses

## ingredients

½ cup butter, at room temperature

¼ cup superfine sugar

2 tablespoons unsweetened cocoa powder

1¼ cups self-rising flour

*Filling*

¼ cup butter, at room temperature

¾ cup confectioners' sugar

a few drops peppermint extract

green and pink food coloring (optional)

## what to do

1 • Set the oven to 350°F.

2 • Put the butter and sugar in the large bowl and beat with the wooden spoon or electric mixer until light and fluffy.

• Sift in the cocoa powder and flour and mix together until smooth, squeezing with your hands when the dough becomes too stiff to stir.

3 • Take teaspoonfuls of the dough, roll into 20 balls and put on the ungreased baking sheets, leaving a little space in between to allow them to spread during cooking.

3

3

- Flatten the cookies slightly with the back of the fork then bake for 10 minutes until they are lightly browned.
- Allow to cool on the baking sheets.

4
- Meanwhile, make the filling by beating together the butter, confectioners' sugar, and peppermint extract in one of the smaller bowls until smooth. Spoon half the frosting into another bowl and, if you like, mix a few drops of green food coloring into one half and a little pink food coloring into the rest in the other bowl.
- Spread 5 of the cookies with the green filling and 5 with the pink then top with the remaining cookies. They can be stored in an airtight container for up to 2 days.

## tip

★ If you are short of time serve the cookies without the filling.

★ If you are not a fan of peppermint leave it out of the frosting or add a little grated orange zest instead.

# chunky chocolate and oat cookies

makes 20

## equipment

pastry brush
2 baking sheets
kitchen scale, measuring cups and spoons
plastic bag
rolling pin
mixing bowl
wooden spoon or electric mixer
teaspoon
spatula
wire rack

## ingredients

oil, for greasing
4 oz white chocolate
4 oz dark chocolate
½ cup butter, at room temperature
½ cup light brown sugar
1 egg, beaten
1 cup whole wheat self-rising flour
1 tablespoon unsweetened cocoa powder
½ cup porridge oats

## what to do

**1**
- Set the oven to 350°F.
- Brush the baking sheets with a little oil.
- Put all the chocolate into the plastic bag and hit with the rolling pin until broken into roughly shaped pieces.

**(2)**
- Put the butter and sugar in the mixing bowl and beat with the wooden spoon or electric mixer until light and fluffy.

(2)

(2)

- Add the egg, flour, cocoa powder, and oats and mix until smooth.
- Stir in the chocolate pieces.

3
- Scoop heaping teaspoons of the mixture onto the oiled baking sheets, leaving a little space in between to allow them to spread during cooking.
- Bake the cookies for 10–13 minutes until they are lightly browned. Allow to harden for 1–2 minutes then loosen with the spatula and transfer to the wire rack to cool completely. The cookies are best eaten on the day they are made.

# sweetheart cookies

## ingredients

oil, for greasing

2 cups all-purpose flour, plus a little extra for dusting the countertop

3 tablespoons custard powder

1/4 cup superfine sugar

2/3 cup butter, at room temperature

1 egg yolk

4 tablespoons seedless raspberry jelly

sifted confectioners' sugar, to decorate

## equipment

pastry brush

2 baking sheets

measuring cups and spoons

large mixing bowl

dull knife

plate

electric mixer (optional)

rolling pin

2 1/2 inch fluted round cookie cutter

1 1/4 inch heart-shaped cookie cutter

small sharp knife

spatula

small sifter

## what to do

**1**
- Set the oven to 325°F.
- Lightly brush the baking sheets with a little oil.

**2**
- Put the flour, custard powder, and sugar in the bowl. Cut the butter into pieces on the plate then add to the bowl. Rub the butter into the flour mixture between your fingertips to make tiny crumbs, or use an electric mixer.

**3**
- Stir in the egg yolk and mix to a smooth dough, first with the dull knife then with your hands when the dough becomes too stiff to stir.

4 • Knead the dough on a surface sprinkled with a little flour then cut it in half and roll out one half until about ¼ inch thick. Stamp out large circles using the round cookie cutter.

• Cut out little hearts from the center of half the circles, using the heart-shaped cutter, and lift out with the end of the small sharp knife. Transfer the rounds to the oiled baking sheets.

• Squeeze the trimmings together and roll out with the remaining dough, stamping out shapes until you have 15 circles with heart-shaped centers cut out and 15 whole circles.

5 • Bake the cookies for 10–12 minutes—slightly less for the heart-stamped ones—until they are pale golden. Loosen the cookies with the spatula and allow to cool on the baking sheets. They can be stored in an airtight container for up to 2 days.

6 • To serve, spread the jelly over the whole cookies, top with the heart-stamped ones then dust with a little sifted confectioners' sugar.

## tip

★ If you don't have a small heart-shaped cutter, use the upturned end of a piping nozzle to cut out tiny circles instead.

# granola munchies

makes 24

## equipment

pastry brush

2 baking sheets

measuring cups and spoons

large mixing bowl

wooden spoon or electric mixer

scissors

teaspoon

spatula

wire rack

## ingredients

oil, for greasing

½ cup butter, at room temperature

½ cup light brown sugar

1 egg

1⅓ cups self-rising flour

½ cup ready-to-eat dried apricots

1 cup "no-added sugar" granola

jumbo oats, to decorate (optional)

## what to do

**1**
- Set the oven to 350°F.
- Brush the baking sheets with a little oil.

**2**
- Put the butter and sugar in the mixing bowl and beat with the wooden spoon or electric mixer until light and fluffy.
- Add the egg and flour and beat until smooth.
- Snip the apricots into small pieces with the scissors then mix into the cookie mixture with the granola.

**3**
- Spoon heaping teaspoonfuls of the mixture onto the oiled baking sheets, leaving a little space in between to allow them to spread during cooking.

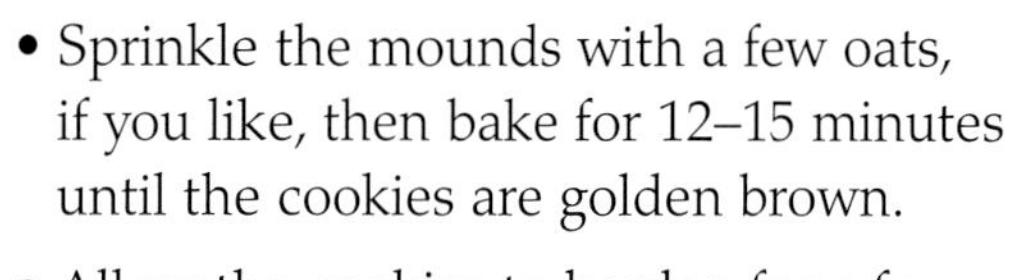

- Sprinkle the mounds with a few oats, if you like, then bake for 12–15 minutes until the cookies are golden brown.
- Allow the cookies to harden for a few minutes, then loosen them with the spatula and transfer to the wire rack to cool completely. They can be stored in an airtight container for up to 2 days.

## tip

★ If you don't have any apricots, then add the same weight of chopped candied cherries, or whole raisins.

# banana, fig, and cranberry slice

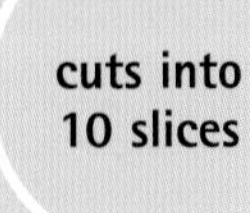

cuts into 10 slices

## equipment

pastry brush

2 lb loaf pan (see page 12)

scissors

waxed paper

kitchen scale and measuring cups and spoons

plate

lemon squeezer

fork

large mixing bowl

wooden spoon

dessertspoon

toothpick

dull knife

wire rack

## ingredients

oil, for greasing

3 small bananas, about 13 oz before peeling

1 tablespoon lemon juice

½ cup butter, at room temperature

¾ cup light brown sugar

2 eggs

1½ cups self-rising flour

1 cup whole wheat self-rising flour

½ cup dried figs

½ cup dried cranberries

2 tablespoons sunflower seeds

## what to do

**1**
- Set the oven to 350°F.
- Brush the loaf pan with a little oil, then cut a piece of waxed paper to cover the base and up the 2 longest sides. Place in the pan and brush with a little extra oil.

**2**
- Peel the bananas then mash them on the plate with the lemon juice, using the fork.

3

3

3
- Put the butter and sugar in the mixing bowl and beat with the wooden spoon until light and fluffy.
- Add the mashed banana, eggs, and flours and beat together until smooth.
- Snip the figs into small pieces with the scissors then add to the banana mixture with the cranberries and stir together.

4
- Spoon the mixture into the pan, smooth flat and sprinkle with the sunflower seeds.
- Bake for 1 hour until the cake is well risen and golden brown, the top has cracked slightly, and a toothpick comes out cleanly.
- Allow the cake to cool in the pan for 30 minutes, then loosen the sides with the dull knife and turn it out onto the wire rack. Remove the lining paper and let cool. Cut into thick slices to serve.

# malted gingerbread squares

## equipment

pastry brush

8 inch square deep cake pan

scissors

waxed paper

measuring cups, spoons, and jug

medium saucepan

wooden spoon

fork

mixing bowl

toothpick

dull knife

wire rack

## ingredients

oil, for greasing

½ cup butter

½ cup dark brown sugar

⅓ cup barley malt extract

⅓ cup light corn syrup

⅔ cup lowfat milk

2 eggs

1⅓ cups self-rising flour

1¼ cups whole wheat all-purpose flour

1 teaspoon baking soda

4 teaspoons ground ginger

rye flakes or jumbo porridge oats, for sprinkling (optional)

## what to do

**1** • Set the oven to 350°F.

• Lightly brush the pan with a little oil, line the base with waxed paper and brush this lightly with a little extra oil.

**(2)** • Put the butter, sugar, malt extract, and syrup into the saucepan and heat gently, stirring from time to time with the wooden spoon until the butter has melted, then take off the heat.

- Beat the milk and eggs in the jug using the fork.
- Mix all the dry ingredients in the bowl.

3 • Add the dry ingredients to the saucepan. Beat until smooth. Add the milk mixture, little by little, and beat until smooth.

4 • Pour the mixture into the lined pan. Sprinkle with a few rye flakes or oats, if you like, and bake for 35–40 minutes until the cake is well risen and deep brown, and a toothpick comes out cleanly when pushed into the center of the cake.

- Allow the cake to cool in the pan for 30 minutes, then loosen the sides with the dull knife and turn out onto the wire rack. Remove the lining paper and let cool completely. Cut into 16 squares to serve. The gingerbread can be stored in an airtight container for up to 1 week.

# coconut, cherry, and lime cake

cuts into
15–18 slices

## equipment

pastry brush

7 inch square deep cake pan

scissors

waxed paper

measuring cups and spoons

large, medium, and small mixing bowls

wooden spoon

strainer

paper towels

small sharp knife

cutting board

grater

toothpick and dull knife

wire rack

sifter

## ingredients

oil, for greasing

1 cup butter, at room temperature

1 cup superfine sugar

4 eggs

2 cups self-rising flour

$1\frac{2}{3}$ cups candied cherries

1 cup shredded coconut

grated zest of 2 limes

*To finish*

$\frac{2}{3}$ cup candied cherries

$1\frac{1}{4}$ cups confectioners' sugar

squeezed juice of 1 lime

2 tablespoons shredded coconut

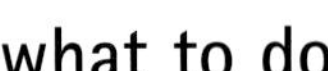

## what to do

**1**
- Set the oven to 350°F.
- Brush the pan with a little oil, line the base with a square of waxed paper and brush this lightly with a little extra oil.

**2**
- Put the butter and sugar into the large mixing bowl and beat with the wooden spoon until light and fluffy.
- Put the eggs in the medium bowl and beat with the fork. Add alternate spoonfuls of egg and then flour to the

butter mixture and keep adding and beating until everything has been added.

3 • Put the cherries in a strainer, rinse under the cold tap then pat dry with paper towels. Cut them into quarters on the cutting board then put them in the small bowl and toss with the coconut and lime zest.

• Add to the ingredients in the large mixing bowl and stir together gently.

**4** • Spoon the mixture into the lined pan and smooth flat with the back of the wooden spoon.

• Bake the cake for 45–55 minutes until it is well risen and golden brown, and a toothpick comes out cleanly when pushed into the center of the cake.

• Leave the cake to cool in the pan for 10 minutes, then loosen the sides with the dull knife and turn out on to the wire rack. Remove the lining paper and allow to cool completely.

5 • To decorate, cut the cherries into halves. Sift the confectioners' sugar into the washed medium bowl then gradually mix in enough lime juice to make a smooth icing.

• Spoon the icing onto the top of the cake and spread with the back of the spoon so that a little runs down the sides.

• Arrange the halved cherries on top of the cake in a heart shape and sprinkle the cake with the coconut. Leave for 30 minutes for the icing to harden. Cut the cake into slices to serve.

5

# tropical fruit cake

## ingredients

oil, for greasing

7½ oz can sliced pineapple

2 cups dried ready-to-eat tropical fruits

⅔ cup candied cherries

¾ cup butter, at room temperature

¾ cup superfine sugar

3 eggs

2 cups all-purpose flour

⅔ cup shredded coconut

## equipment

pastry brush

7 inch round deep cake pan

scissors

waxed paper

strainer

1 large and 2 small bowls

cutting board

paper towels

small sharp knife

measuring cups

wooden spoon

fork

dessertspoon

toothpick

dull knife

wire rack

## what to do

1 • Set the oven to 325°F.

• Lightly brush the pan with a little oil, line the base with a circle of waxed paper and brush this lightly with a little extra oil.

• Tip the canned pineapple into the strainer set over a small bowl and drain well. Tip out onto the cutting board, pat dry with a piece of paper towel then cut into small pieces.

• Cut or snip the tropical fruits and the cherries into pieces using the sharp knife or scissors.

2 • Put the butter and sugar in the large mixing bowl and beat with the wooden spoon until light and fluffy.

- Put the eggs in a small bowl and beat with the fork.
- Gradually mix a spoonful of beaten egg then a spoonful of flour into the butter mixture and keep adding and mixing until both have been added and the mixture is smooth.

**3**
- Stir in the pineapple and tropical fruits then the cherries and coconut.
- Spoon the mixture into the lined pan and smooth flat with the back of the spoon.

**4**
- Cook the cake for about 1–1¼ hours until it is golden brown, and a toothpick comes out cleanly when pushed into the center of the cake. Cover loosely with foil after 40 minutes if needed.
- Allow the cake to cool in the pan for 10 minutes, then loosen the sides with the dull knife and turn out onto the wire rack. Remove the lining paper and leave to cool completely. Cut into slices to serve. The cake can be stored in an airtight container for up to 1 week.

# apple and madeira cake

cuts into 8–10 slices

## equipment

8 inch deep round cake pan
nonstick parchment paper
scissors
vegetable peeler
small knife
cutting board
grater
measuring cups
large and small mixing bowls
wooden spoon or electric mixer
fork
toothpick

## ingredients

2 dessert apples
1 orange
¾ cup soft margarine
¾ cup superfine sugar
3 eggs
2¼ cups self-rising flour
little superfine sugar, to decorate

## what to do

1 • Set the oven to 325°F.

• Line the cake pan, base and sides, with nonstick parchment paper (see page 12).

• Peel the apples, cut them into quarters, then cut away the cores. Cut the apples into small pieces.

• Finely grate the orange, then cut two slices and cut each one in half. (Eat the rest of the orange.)

2 • Put the margarine and sugar in the large mixing bowl and beat with the wooden spoon or electric mixer until light and fluffy.

- Put the eggs into the small bowl and mix together with a fork.
- Add a spoonful of egg then a spoonful of flour to the margarine mixture and mix until smooth. Continue adding alternate spoonfuls until both have been added and the mixture is smooth.

3
- Stir the apple pieces and grated orange zest into the cake mixture.
- Spoon the mixture into the lined pan and spread the top flat with the back of the spoon.
- Arrange the halved orange slices in the center to make a pattern.
- Bake the cake for about 1 hour until it is well risen and golden brown and a toothpick comes out cleanly when pushed into the center of the cake.

4
- Carefully take the cake out of the pan and put it on the wire rack. Remove the lining paper and allow to cool completely.
- Sprinkle with a little extra sugar, then cut into slices to serve. The cake can be stored in an airtight container for up to 1 week.

cuts into 10 slices

## equipment

measuring cups, spoons, and jug
small saucepan
medium mixing bowl
pastry brush
2 lb loaf pan (see page 12)
scissors
waxed paper
grater
wooden spoon
dessertspoon
toothpick
dull knife
wire rack

# apple and raisin loaf

## ingredients

$1\frac{3}{4}$ cups apple juice
2 cups golden raisins
oil, for greasing
2 crisp dessert apples (such as Granny Smith)
2 tablespoons chopped mixed candied peel
$\frac{1}{2}$ cup superfine sugar
$2\frac{1}{2}$ cups self-rising flour
1 egg
1 large piece candied citron peel, to decorate (optional)

## what to do

**1**
- Pour the apple juice into the pan and bring to a boil. Put the raisins in the mixing bowl then pour over the hot apple juice.
- Allow to soak for 4 hours or overnight.

**2**
- Set the oven to 325°F.
- Brush the loaf pan with a little oil. Cut a piece of waxed paper to fit over the base and up the 2 longest sides. Place in the pan and brush with a little extra oil.

**3**
- Coarsely grate the apples down to the cores then add the apple to the raisins.
- Add the chopped peel, sugar, flour, and egg to the raisins and mix with the wooden spoon.

1

3

## tip

★ Citron peel is a mix of candied orange, lime, and lemon peel. The pieces are quarter sections of the whole fruit zest. It is not the same as chopped mixed peel.

- Spoon into the lined pan and smooth flat with the back of the metal spoon.

**4** • Decorate the top of the cake with snipped strips of citron peel, if using.

- Bake the cake for about 1¼ hours until it is well risen and golden brown, and a toothpick pushed into the center comes out cleanly. Loosely cover it with foil if it is browning too fast.

**5** • Leave the cake to cool in the pan for 30 minutes, then loosen the sides with the dull knife and turn out onto the wire rack. Remove the lining paper and allow to cool completely.

- Serve cut into thick slices. It can be stored in an airtight container for up to 3 days.

# rippled date and orange loaf

cuts into 10 slices

## equipment

pastry brush

2 lb loaf pan (see page 12)

scissors

waxed paper

grater

lemon squeezer

measuring cups and spoons

small saucepan

large mixing bowl

wooden spoon or electric mixer

dessertspoon

dull knife

toothpick

kitchen foil

wire rack

## ingredients

oil, for greasing

1 orange

1 1/3 cups ready-chopped pitted dates

6 tablespoons water

2 cups self-rising flour

1/2 teaspoon baking powder

2/3 cup superfine sugar

2/3 cup soft margarine

3 eggs

## what to do

1 • Set the oven to 350°F.

• Lightly brush the loaf pan with a little oil, then cut a piece of waxed paper long enough to go over the base and up the 2 longest sides. Place in the pan and brush lightly with a little extra oil.

• Finely grate the zest from the orange. Cut it in half then squeeze the juice.

2 • Put the orange juice, dates, and water in the saucepan and heat gently without a lid for 5 minutes until the dates are soft.

• Allow to cool for 10 minutes.

1

3

(3) • Put the orange zest in the mixing bowl. Add all the remaining ingredients except the date mixture. Beat with the wooden spoon or electric mixer until smooth.

- Spoon one-third of the cake mixture into the lined pan and smooth flat with the back of the metal spoon.
- Dot half the date mixture over the cake mixture then smooth flat with the knife.
- Repeat one more time then cover with the last of the cake mixture.

**4** • Bake for about 1 hour until the cake is well risen, cracked on top and golden brown. A toothpick pushed into the center should come out cleanly. Look at the cake after 30–40 minutes; loosely cover it with foil if it is browning too fast.

- Carefully loosen the sides of the cake with the dull knife and turn out onto the wire rack. Remove the lining paper and leave to cool before cutting into slices to serve. The cake can be stored in an airtight container for up to 3 days.

# farmhouse fruit cake

## equipment

scissors

nonstick parchment paper

7 inch round deep cake pan

measuring cups and spoons

1 large and 2 small mixing bowls

wooden spoon or electric mixer

fork

dessertspoon

small sharp knife

cutting board

toothpick

kitchen foil

dull knife

wire rack

## ingredients

½ cup butter, at room temperature

½ cup light brown sugar

2 eggs

1½ cups self-rising flour

½ teaspoon ground cinnamon

a little grated nutmeg

1⅔ cups mixed dried fruit

*To decorate*

4 candied cherries

1 large piece candied citron peel (see "Tip," page 73)

## what to do

**1**
- Set the oven to 325°F.
- Line the cake pan, base and sides, with nonstick parchment paper (see page 12).

**2**
- Put the butter and sugar in the large mixing bowl and beat with the wooden spoon or electric mixer until smooth.
- Beat the eggs in a smaller bowl with the fork and mix the flour and spices in the other small bowl.
- Gradually mix alternate spoonfuls of egg and flour into the butter mixture until both have been added and the mixture is smooth.
- Stir in the dried fruit.

3 • Spoon the mixture into the lined pan and smooth flat with the back of the spoon.

• Cut the cherries in half and the citron peel into triangles, then arrange over the top of the cake.

• Bake the cake for about 1¼ hours or until it is well risen and browned, and a toothpick comes out cleanly when pushed into the center of the cake.

4 • Leave the cake to cool in the pan for 30 minutes, then loosen the sides with the dull knife and turn out onto the wire rack. Remove the lining paper and allow to cool completely. The cake can be stored in an airtight container for up to 1 week.

## tip

★ Check on the cake from time to time during cooking and cover it loosely with kitchen foil if the top seems to be browning too quickly.

# sesame and maple syrup oaties

## equipment

scissors

nonstick parchment paper

8 inch square shallow cake pan

measuring cups and spoons

medium saucepan

wooden spoon

dessertspoon

dull knife

cutting board

large sharp knife

## ingredients

1 cup butter

1 cup brown sugar

5 tablespoons maple syrup or light corn syrup

¼ cup sesame seeds, plus 1 extra tablespoon for sprinkling

2½ cups oats

## what to do

**1** • Set the oven to 350°F.

• Cut a square of nonstick parchment paper a little larger than the pan, snip into the corners and press the paper into the pan.

**2** • Put the butter, sugar, and syrup in the saucepan and heat gently, stirring from time to time with the wooden spoon, until completely melted.

**3** • Take the saucepan off the heat and stir in the sesame seeds and oats.

• Spoon the mixture into the lined pan and press flat with the back of the metal spoon.

- Sprinkle with the extra 1 tablespoon of sesame seeds.

**4**
- Bake for 20–25 minutes until golden brown and just beginning to darken around the edges of the pan. Allow to cool for 10 minutes.
- Mark into squares with the dull knife and leave to harden and cool completely.

**5**
- Lift out of the pan with the paper, peel off the paper and put on the cutting board. Cut into 9 pieces to serve. The oaties can be stored in an airtight container for up to 3 days.

# triple choc brownies

## ingredients

5 oz dark chocolate

½ cup butter, at room temperature

3 oz white chocolate

3 oz milk chocolate

3 eggs

1 cup superfine sugar

1⅓ cups self-rising flour

1 teaspoon baking powder

## equipment

scissors

nonstick parchment paper

small roasting pan (see page 12)

medium saucepan

large and medium bowls

kitchen scale, measuring cups, and spoons

dull knife

plate

plastic bag

rolling pin

electric beater

large metal spoon

sifter

cutting board

large sharp knife

## what to do

**1**
- Set the oven to 350°F.
- Cut a piece of nonstick parchment paper a little larger than the pan, snip into the corners and press the paper into the pan.

**2**
- Half-fill the saucepan with water, bring just to a boil then turn off the heat and place the large bowl on top.
- Break the dark chocolate into pieces and cut the butter into pieces on the plate, then add both to the large bowl. Leave for 5 minutes or so until melted.

**(3)**
- Put the white and milk chocolate in the plastic bag and hit with the rolling pin until broken into small pieces.

(5)

4 • Beat the eggs and sugar in the second bowl for 5 minutes using the electric beater until thick and very frothy.

(5) • Pour the melted chocolate and butter mixture over the top and mix in very gently using the metal spoon.

• Sift the flour and baking powder over the top then carefully fold in.

6 • Pour the mixture into the lined pan. Sprinkle with the white and milk chocolate pieces.

• Bake for 20–25 minutes until the top is crusty and the center still wobbles slightly. Allow to cool and harden in the pan.

7 • Lift the paper and cake out of the pan, remove the paper and put the cake on the cutting board. Cut into 18 pieces. The brownies can be stored in an airtight container for up to 2 days.

## tip

★ Melt the white chocolate and drizzle it from a spoon over the top of the cooked brownies instead of adding it to the raw mixture, if you prefer.

# toffee apple squares

## ingredients

oil, for greasing

$^3/_4$ cup soft margarine

$^3/_4$ cup light brown sugar, plus 2 tablespoons for sprinkling

3 eggs

2 cups self-rising flour

1 teaspoon vanilla extract

4 oz hard toffees, unwrapped

3 dessert apples

$^1/_4$ cup butter

## equipment

pastry brush

small roasting pan (see page 12)

scissors

waxed paper

kitchen scale, measuring cups and spoons

large and small bowls

wooden spoon

fork

plastic bag

rolling pin

large and small knife

cutting board

vegetable peeler

dessertspoon

small saucepan

toothpick and wire rack

## what to do

**1**
- Set the oven to 350°F.
- Brush the pan with a little oil. Cut a piece of waxed paper to fit over the base and partway up the 2 longest sides. Place in the pan and brush with a little extra oil.

**2**
- Put the margarine and sugar in the large bowl and beat with the wooden spoon until smooth.
- Put the eggs in the small bowl and beat with the fork. Gradually beat a little of the eggs then a little of the flour into the margarine mixture and keep adding and beating until both have been added and the mixture is smooth. Stir in the vanilla extract.

3
- Put the toffees in the plastic bag and hit with the rolling pin until broken into chunky pieces.
- Quarter, core and peel the apples. Cut 4 quarters into small pieces and thinly slice the rest.
- Stir half the toffees and the small pieces of apple into the cake mixture then spoon into the lined pan and smooth flat.
- Arrange the apple slices neatly in rows over the top.
- Melt the butter in the saucepan on the stove. Brush the melted butter over the top of the apples, sprinkle with the rest of the toffees and the extra 2 tablespoons of the sugar.

4
- Bake the cake for 40–45 minutes until it is well risen and golden brown, and a toothpick comes out cleanly when pushed into the center of the cake.
- Leave the cake to cool in the pan then lift onto the wire rack. Peel off the paper and cut into 15 squares. Serve warm or cold. The squares can be stored in an airtight container for up to 2 days.

# date and apple bars

makes 12

## equipment

scissors

nonstick parchment paper

8 inch square shallow cake pan

small sharp knife

cutting board

vegetable peeler

measuring cups and spoons

small and medium saucepans

wooden spoon

dessertspoon

dull knife

large sharp knife

## ingredients

1 dessert apple

1 cup ready-chopped pitted dates

4 tablespoons water

⅔ cup butter

⅓ cup light brown sugar

3 tablespoons light corn syrup

¾ cup whole wheat all-purpose or granary flour

2⅔ cups "no-added sugar" granola

3 tablespoons sunflower seeds

3 tablespoons pine nuts or roughly chopped almonds or hazelnuts

## what to do

**1**
- Set the oven to 350°F.
- Cut a square of nonstick parchment paper a little larger than the pan, snip into the corners and press the paper into the pan.

**2**
- Quarter, core, and peel the apple then cut into small pieces.
- Put the apple and dates in the small saucepan with the water, cover and cook gently for 5 minutes until softened.

**3**
- Put the butter, sugar, and syrup into the medium saucepan and heat gently, stirring from time to time with the wooden spoon

4

4

until the butter has melted and the sugar has dissolved.

- Take the pan off the heat and stir in the flour, granola, sunflower seeds, and nuts.

4 • Spoon three-quarters of the mixture into the lined pan and press flat with the back of the metal spoon.

- Spoon the date mixture on top, draining off any remaining water.
- Top with spoonfuls of the remaining granola mixture—don't worry if the date mixture shows through in places.

**5** • Bake for 25–30 minutes until it is a mid-brown color. Allow to cool and harden for 10 minutes then mark into 12 bars. Leave in the pan to cool completely.

- Lift out of the pan with the paper, peel off the paper and cut into bars on the cutting board. The bars can be stored in an airtight container for up to 3 days.

# squashed fly bars

## equipment

pastry brush
small roasting pan (see page 12)
scissors
waxed paper
measuring cups
large mixing bowl
wooden spoon or electric mixer
dessertspoon
dull knife
wire rack
sifter
large sharp knife

## ingredients

oil, for greasing
1 cup soft margarine
1 cup superfine sugar
2 cups self-rising flour
4 eggs
1 cup golden raisins
sifted confectioners' sugar, to decorate

## what to do

1
- Set the oven to 350°F.
- Brush the pan with a little oil. Cut a piece of waxed paper to fit over the base and partway up the 2 longest sides. Place in the pan and brush with a little extra oil.

2
- Put the margarine, sugar, flour, and eggs in the mixing bowl and beat with the wooden spoon or electric mixer for 1–2 minutes until smooth.
- Stir in the golden raisins.

3
- Pour the mixture into the lined pan and smooth flat with the metal spoon.
- Bake the cake for 25–30 minutes until it is well risen and golden brown, and the top springs back when lightly pressed with a fingertip.

4 • Leave the cake to cool in the pan for 10 minutes, then loosen the sides with the dull knife and turn out onto the wire rack. Remove the lining paper and allow to cool completely.

• Decorate with a little sifted confectioners' sugar and cut into 16 bars to serve. The bars can be stored in an airtight container for up to 3 days.

## tip

★ Swap the golden raisins for chocolate dots or diced milk chocolate, if you like.

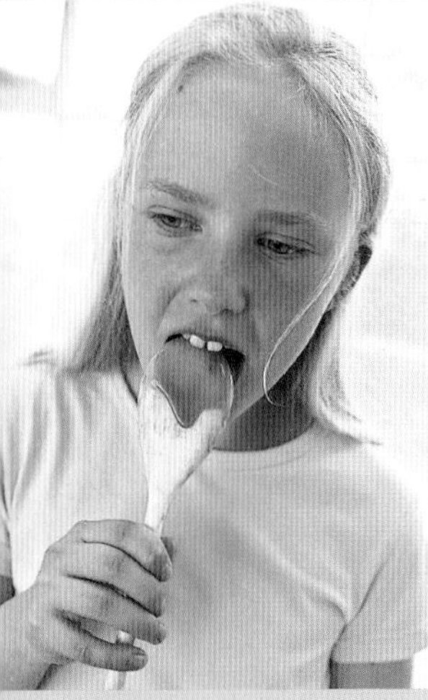

# millionaire's shortbread

## equipment

pastry brush

small roasting pan (see page 12)

kitchen scale and measuring cups and spoons

large and medium mixing bowls

dull knife

plate

small saucepan

wooden spoon

dessertspoon

large sharp knife

## ingredients

oil, for greasing

2 cups all-purpose flour

3 tablespoons cornstarch

¼ cup superfine sugar

¾ cup butter, at room temperature

*Topping*

2 tablespoons light corn syrup

⅓ cup butter

⅓ cup light brown sugar

3 tablespoons heavy cream

3 oz dark or milk chocolate

3 oz white chocolate (optional)

## what to do

**1**
- Set the oven to 350°F.
- Lightly brush the pan with a little oil.

**(2)**
- Put the flour, cornstarch, and sugar in the large mixing bowl.
- Cut the butter into pieces on the plate then add to the bowl. Rub the butter into the flour mixture between your fingertips to make tiny crumbs.
- Squeeze the crumbs together then tip the mixture into the oiled pan and press flat with your hands.

**(3)**
- Bake the shortbread for 20–25 minutes until it is pale golden.

- When the shortbread is almost ready, put the syrup, butter, and sugar in the saucepan and heat until the butter has melted. Boil for 1 minute. Stir in the cream and cook for 30 seconds.
- Pour over the hot shortbread, smooth flat then allow to cool and set.

4
- To finish, break the dark or milk chocolate into pieces and put in the second bowl. Put this over a saucepan of just boiled water and leave for 4–5 minutes until melted.
- Drizzle spoonfuls of the melted chocolate in wiggly scribble-like lines over the set topping. Chill for 15 minutes.
- Melt the white chocolate, if using, in the same way as the dark then drizzle over the top. Chill until set. Cut the shortbread into 18 pieces and lift out of the pan.

# mini birthday cake squares

makes 24

## equipment

pastry brush

small roasting pan (see page 12)

scissors

waxed paper

measuring cups and spoons

1 large, 1 medium, and 2 small mixing bowls

grater

wooden spoon

dessertspoon

dull knife

wire rack

large cutting board

large sharp knife

## ingredients

oil, for greasing

1 cup soft margarine

1 cup superfine sugar

2 cups self-rising flour

4 eggs

grated zest of 1 lemon or 1 small orange

*To finish*

½ cup butter, at room temperature

1⅔ cups confectioners' sugar

2–4 teaspoons milk

a few drops blue, orange, and pink food coloring

24 candles and candle holders

selection of candies (such as mini candy-coated chocolate candies or mini marshmallows)

sugar strands

## what to do

**1**
- Set the oven to 350°F.
- Brush the pan with a little oil, line the base with a rectangle of waxed paper and brush this with a little extra oil.

**2**
- Put all the cake ingredients in the large bowl and beat with the wooden spoon.
- Spoon into the pan and smooth flat.

**3**
- Bake the cake for 25–30 minutes until it is well risen and golden brown, and the top springs back when lightly pressed.

- Leave the cake to cool in the pan for about 10 minutes, then loosen the sides with the dull knife and turn out onto the wire rack. Carefully remove the lining paper and leave the cake to cool completely.

4
- To make the frosting, beat the butter in the medium bowl with a little of the confectioners' sugar (there is no need to sift it first), then gradually mix in the rest, a few spoonfuls at a time, along with enough milk to make a smooth spreadable frosting.
- Divide the frosting into 3 and place two of the thirds in the small bowls. Color one-third of the frosting pale blue, one-third pale orange and the rest pale pink.
- Put the cake on the large cutting board and cut into 3 pieces. Spread a different colored frosting over each piece of cake using the dull knife. Cut into 24 small pieces with a large sharp knife.
- Put a candle holder and candle in the center of each piece then arrange the candies and sugar strands around it. Store in an airtight container for up to 2 days.

# scottish shortbread

makes 8

## equipment

measuring cups
large mixing bowl
dull knife
plate
electric mixer (optional)
8 inch fluted-edged, removable-bottomed tart pan
fork
large sharp knife

## ingredients

1½ cups all-purpose flour
½ cup butter, at room temperature
¼ cup superfine sugar, plus a little extra for sprinkling

## what to do

**1** • Set the oven to 325°F.

• Put the flour in the mixing bowl. Cut the butter into pieces on the plate then add to the flour along with the sugar.

**2** • Rub the butter into the flour mixture between your fingertips to make tiny crumbs, or use an electric mixer.

• Squeeze the crumbs together with your hands until they stick together.

**3** • Tip the mixture into the pan (there is no need to grease it first) and press flat using your hands.

• Decorate all around the edge of the shortbread by pressing your finger into the edge. Prick the middle with the fork and sprinkle with a little extra sugar.

**4** • Bake the shortbread for 20–25 minutes until it is pale golden.

2

3

- Take out of the oven and mark into 8 triangular-shaped pieces. Allow the shortbread to cool in the pan.
- Cut the shortbread right through and lift out of the pan. These can be stored in an airtight container for up to 5 days.

## tip

★ If you don't have a tart pan then press the shortbread into a round on a baking sheet.

# frosted gingerbread and banana slices

## equipment

pastry brush
small roasting pan (see page 12)
scissors
waxed paper
measuring cups and spoons
medium saucepan
wooden spoon
plate
fork
2 small mixing bowls
dessertspoon
dull knife
wire rack
sifter
large sharp knife

## ingredients

oil, for greasing
½ cup butter
½ cup light corn syrup
½ cup light brown sugar
2 bananas, each about 6 oz before peeling
2 eggs
2 tablespoons milk
2 cups self-rising flour
2 teaspoons ground ginger
½ teaspoon baking soda

*To finish*

1⅔ cups confectioners' sugar
5–6 teaspoons water
few drops pink food coloring (optional)
sugar strands, to decorate

## what to do

**1** • Set the oven to 350°F.

• Lightly brush the pan with a little oil, line the base with a rectangle of waxed paper and brush this lightly with a little extra oil.

2 • Put the butter, syrup, and sugar in the saucepan. Heat gently, stirring occasionally with the wooden spoon until melted.

• Meanwhile, peel then mash the bananas on the plate using the fork.

• Put the eggs and milk in one of the small bowls and mix together with the fork.

• Put the flour, ginger, and baking soda in the other small bowl and mix with the dessertspoon.

**3** • Take the pan off the heat, add the flour mixture and bananas and beat until smooth. Add the egg and milk mixture and mix well.

• Pour the cake mixture into the lined pan. Smooth flat with the back of the spoon.

**4** • Bake the gingerbread for 20–25 minutes until it is well risen and golden brown, and the top springs back when lightly pressed with a fingertip.

• Leave the gingerbread to cool in the pan for 10 minutes, then loosen the sides with the dull knife and turn out onto the wire rack. Remove the lining paper and allow to cool completely.

5 • To make the frosting, sift the confectioners' sugar into a clean bowl. Gradually mix in the water to make a smooth spreadable frosting. Color it pale pink if you'd like.

• Pour the frosting over the top of the cake and smooth flat with the dull knife. Decorate with sugar strands.

• Allow to cool for 30 minutes until the frosting has set, then cut the gingerbread into 16 bars. The slices can be stored in an airtight container for up to 3 days.

# carrot, honey, and raisin squares

## equipment

pastry brush

small roasting pan (see page 12)

scissors

waxed paper

kitchen scale, measuring cups, spoons, and jug

vegetable peeler

grater

cutting board

large and medium mixing bowls

fork or balloon whisk

dessertspoon

dull knife

wire rack

lemon squeezer

large sharp knife

## ingredients

oil, for greasing

3 carrots, 7 oz in total before peeling

⅔ cup sunflower oil

3 eggs

⅓ cup honey

¼ cup light brown sugar

1¾ cups whole wheat self-rising flour

2 teaspoons baking powder

⅔ cup golden raisins

*To finish*

½ orange

½ cup butter, at room temperature

1⅔ cups confectioners' sugar

large and small candy-coated chocolate candies, to decorate

## what to do

(1)
- Set the oven to 350°F.
- Brush the pan with a little oil, line the base with a rectangle of waxed paper and brush this lightly with a little extra oil.
- Peel then grate the carrots onto the board.

(2)
- Put the oil, eggs, honey, and sugar in the large mixing bowl and mix together using the fork or whisk.

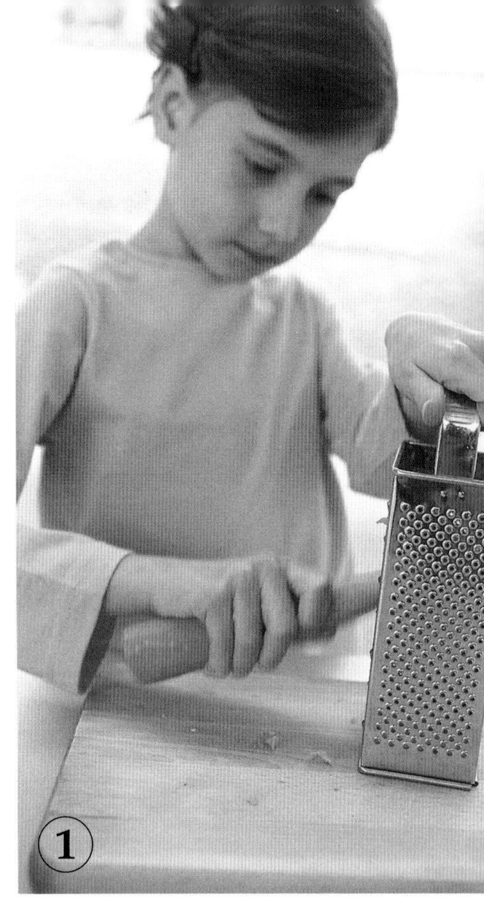

- Add the flour and baking powder and mix well, then stir in the grated carrots and the raisins with the metal spoon.
- Pour the cake mixture into the lined pan and smooth flat.

**3**
- Bake the cake for 20–25 minutes until it is well risen and golden brown, and the top springs back when lightly pressed.
- Leave the cake to cool in the pan for 10 minutes, then loosen the sides with the dull knife and turn out onto the wire rack. Remove the lining paper and allow to cool completely.

**4**
- To make the frosting, finely grate the orange and squeeze the juice.
- Put the butter in the medium mixing bowl, add the orange zest then gradually mix in the confectioners' sugar and some of the orange juice to make a soft spreadable frosting.
- Spread the frosting over the top of the cake with the dull knife then cut the cake into 15 pieces. Decorate with the candy. The squares can be stored in an airtight container for up to 2 days.

# cherry streusel cake

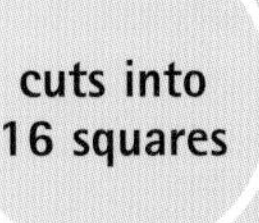

cuts into 16 squares

## equipment

scissors

nonstick parchment paper

8 inch square shallow cake pan

kitchen scale and measuring cups and spoons

large and small mixing bowls

dull knife

plate

electric mixer (optional)

wooden spoon

dessertspoon

strainer

large sharp knife

## ingredients

1½ cups self-rising flour

½ cup butter, at room temperature

⅓ cup superfine sugar

½ cup ground almonds

1 egg

2 tablespoons milk

½ teaspoon almond extract

14 oz can pitted black cherries

¼ cup slivered almonds

## what to do

**1**
- Set the oven to 350°F.
- Cut a square of nonstick parchment paper a little larger than the pan, snip into the corners and press the paper into the pan.

**(2)**
- Put the flour in the large mixing bowl. Cut the butter into pieces on the plate then add to the flour. Rub the butter into the flour between your fingertips to make tiny crumbs, or use an electric mixer.
- Stir in the sugar and ground almonds.
- Measure out 3 oz of the crumb mixture and set aside for the topping in the

(2)

(3)

second bowl. Add the egg, milk, and almond extract to the rest of the mixture and mix together until smooth.

3 • Spoon the soft cake mixture into the lined pan and smooth flat.

• Tip the cherries into the strainer set over the empty small bowl and drain away the liquid, then spoon the cherries on top of the cake mixture.

• Sprinkle with the reserved crumbs and the slivered almonds.

**4** • Bake the cake for 25–30 minutes until it is well risen and the topping is pale golden.

• Leave the cake to cool in the pan, then loosen the sides and lift out, holding the edges of the paper. Peel away the paper then cut into 16 squares. Store the cake in an airtight container for up to 2 days.

## equipment

pastry brush

two 8 inch layer cake pans

scissors

waxed paper

kitchen scale and measuring cups and spoons

grater

large, medium, and small mixing bowls

wooden spoon

2 dessertspoons

dull knife

wire rack

serving plate

sifter

# strawberry and mascarpone layer cake

## ingredients

oil, for greasing

$^{3}/_{4}$ cup soft margarine

$^{3}/_{4}$ cup superfine sugar

$1^{1}/_{2}$ cups self-rising flour

1 teaspoon baking powder

grated zest of 1 lemon

3 eggs

*To finish*

6 oz low-fat mascarpone cheese

2 tablespoons confectioners' sugar, plus a little extra for dusting

$2^{2}/_{3}$ cups strawberries, stalks removed

3 tablespoons strawberry jelly

## what to do

**1** • Set the oven to 350°F.

• Brush the pans with a little oil, line the bases with circles of waxed paper and brush these with a little extra oil.

**(2)** • Put all the cake ingredients in the large bowl and beat with the wooden spoon.

- Divide the mixture equally between the 2 lined pans and smooth flat with the back of a metal spoon.

3
- Bake the cakes for about 20 minutes until they are well risen and golden brown, and the tops spring back when lightly pressed.
- Leave the cakes to cool in the pans for 5 minutes, then loosen the sides with the dull knife and turn out onto the wire rack. Remove the lining paper and allow to cool completely.

4
- To make the filling, put the mascarpone cheese and confectioners' sugar in the medium bowl and beat together until soft.

(5)
- Put one of the cakes on the serving plate and spread with the cheese mixture.
- Keep back 4 strawberries for the decoration and slice the rest. Mix these with the jelly in the small bowl then spoon on top of the cheese mixture. Carefully put the second cake on top.
- Decorate with the reserved strawberries, cut in halves (keeping them in place with a little mascarpone, if necessary) and a little extra sifted confectioners' sugar. The cake is best eaten on the day it is made.

# peach melba cake

cuts into 10–12 slices

## equipment

pastry brush

8 inch round springform pan

scissors

waxed paper

kitchen scale and measuring cups

small sharp knife

cutting board

grater

large and small bowls

wooden spoon

fork

dessertspoon

teaspoon

toothpick

wire rack

serving plate

## ingredients

oil, for greasing

3 peaches, about 12 oz in total

1 cup butter, at room temperature

1 cup superfine sugar

grated zest of 1 lemon

3 eggs

1¾ cups self-rising flour

1 cup raspberries

5 oz full-fat cream cheese

sifted confectioners' sugar, to decorate

## what to do

**1** • Set the oven to 325°F.

• Brush the pan with a little oil, line the base with waxed paper and brush this with a little extra oil.

• Cut the peaches in half, cut out the pits and then thinly slice the fruit.

**2** • Beat the butter, sugar, and zest in the large bowl with the wooden spoon until fluffy.

• Beat the eggs in the small bowl with the fork. Slowly add a little egg to the butter mixture then some flour, beating well after each addition. Continue until both have been added. Mix for 1–2 minutes.

• Spoon half the cake mixture into the lined pan and smooth flat.

3

3

3
- Cover with half the peach slices and half the raspberries then dot all the cream cheese over the top, using the teaspoon.
- Spoon the rest of the cake mixture on top and gently smooth flat.
- Arrange the remaining peach slices and raspberries over the top.

4
- Bake the cake for about 1 hour 10 minutes to 1 hour 25 minutes until it is well risen and a toothpick comes out cleanly when pushed into the center of the cake.
- Leave the cake to cool in the pan for 15 minutes. Loosen the sides with the dull knife, then release the cake and transfer to the wire rack. Remove the lining paper and allow to cool completely.
- Dust the cake with a little sifted confectioners' sugar.

# chocolate fudge squares

## equipment

pastry brush

8 inch square shallow cake pan

scissors

waxed paper

kitchen scale and measuring cups and spoons

large mixing bowl

wooden spoon

dessertspoon

dull knife

wire rack

medium saucepan

large sharp knife

## ingredients

oil, for greasing

¾ cup soft margarine

¾ cup superfine sugar

1⅓ cups self-rising flour

¼ cup unsweetened cocoa powder

½ teaspoon baking powder

3 eggs

*To finish*

2 tablespoons butter

4 oz dark chocolate

3 tablespoons confectioners' sugar

2–3 teaspoons milk

small candies to decorate

## what to do

**1**
- Set the oven to 350°F.
- Brush the pan with a little oil, line the base with waxed paper and brush this lightly with a little extra oil.

**2**
- Put all the cake ingredients in the mixing bowl and beat with the wooden spoon. Spoon into the pan and smooth flat.
- Bake the cake for 25–30 minutes until it is well risen and browned, and the top springs back when lightly pressed.

**3** • Leave the cake to cool in the pan for 10 minutes, then loosen the sides with the dull knife and turn out onto the wire rack. Remove the lining paper and allow to cool completely.

**(4)** • To make the frosting, heat the butter in the saucepan until just melted. Break the chocolate into squares, add to the pan and heat gently until melted.

- Stir in the confectioners' sugar and heat gently until glossy then stir in enough milk to make a thick spreadable frosting. Quickly pour over the top of the cake and spread into an even layer. Decorate with the candies and mark into 16 squares. Let the frosting harden for 30 minutes.
- Cut the cake into the squares and store in an airtight container for up to 2 days.

cuts into 10 slices

## equipment

pastry brush
8 inch round springform pan
scissors
waxed paper
measuring cups and spoons
small, medium, and large mixing bowls
teaspoon
wooden spoon
tablespoon
grater
dull knife
toothpick
wire rack
small saucepan
large plate

# chocolate and orange swirl cake

## ingredients

oil, for greasing
4 teaspoons unsweetened cocoa powder
4 teaspoons boiling water
3/4 cup soft margarine
3/4 cup superfine sugar
1 3/4 cups self-rising flour
3 eggs
grated zest of 1/2 orange

*To finish*
1/4 cup butter
1/4 cup unsweetened cocoa powder
2 cups confectioners' sugar
1–2 tablespoons milk
sugar flowers or chocolate candies (such as segments of chocolate orange or a sliced chocolate bar), to decorate

## what to do

**1** • Set the oven to 350°F.
• Lightly brush the pan with a little oil, line the base with a circle of waxed paper and brush this lightly with a little extra oil.
• Put the cocoa powder in the small bowl, add the boiling water and mix to a paste.

**2** • Put the margarine, sugar, flour, and eggs in the large mixing bowl and beat with the wooden spoon until smooth.

3

3

- Spoon half the mixture into the medium bowl and stir in the cocoa paste.
- Stir the orange zest into the other half of the cake mixture.

3 • Add alternate spoonfuls of the 2 different cake mixtures to the lined pan then run the dull knife through the colors to marble or swirl them together.
- Bake the cake for 35–40 minutes until it is well risen and golden brown, and a toothpick comes out cleanly when pushed into the center of the cake.

4 • Leave the cake to cool in the pan for 15 minutes. Loosen the sides with the dull knife, then release the cake and transfer to the wire rack. Remove the lining paper and allow to cool completely.

5 • To make the frosting, put the butter in the small saucepan and heat until melted.
- Stir in the cocoa powder and cook for 1 minute.
- Take off the heat. Stir in the confectioners' sugar. Return to the burner and heat for 1 minute until glossy. Stir in enough milk to make a smooth spreadable frosting.
- Transfer the cake to a wire rack set over a large plate. Spoon the frosting over the top, then smooth evenly with the knife. Decorate with sugar flowers and allow to harden for 30 minutes before slicing. Store in an airtight container for up to 2 days.

# carrot and banana layer cake

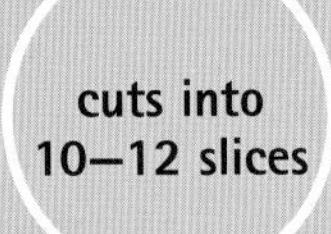

cuts into 10–12 slices

## equipment

pastry brush

8 inch round deep cake pan

scissors

waxed paper

kitchen scale, measuring spoons, cups, and jug

large and small bowls

fork

wooden spoon

grater

2 plates

toothpick

dull knife

wire rack

large serrated knife

lemon squeezer

serving plate

## ingredients

oil, for greasing

¾ cup light brown sugar

¾ cup sunflower oil

4 eggs

2 carrots, about 7 oz in total, scrubbed

1 small banana, about 5 oz before peeling

½ cup golden raisins (optional)

1½ cups self-rising flour

1½ cups whole wheat self-rising flour

1 teaspoon ground cinnamon

1 teaspoon baking powder

*To finish*

13 oz full-fat cream cheese

1¼ cups confectioners' sugar

grated zest of 1 orange

2 tablespoons orange juice

a few banana chips and a few orange slices, to decorate

## what to do

**1** • Set the oven to 350°F.

• Lightly brush the pan with a little oil, line the base with a circle of waxed paper and brush this lightly with a little extra oil.

**2** • Put the sugar, oil, and eggs in the large bowl and beat with the fork until well mixed.

- Coarsely grate the carrots onto a plate.
- Peel then mash the banana on the other plate using the fork.

3
- Add the grated carrots and mashed banana to the egg mixture along with the golden raisins, if using, and mix together.
- Add the flours, cinnamon, and baking powder and mix together.
- Pour the mixture into the lined pan and smooth with the back of the spoon.

④
- Bake the cake for about 1 hour until it is well risen and golden brown, and a toothpick comes out cleanly when pushed into the center of the cake.
- Leave the cake to cool in the pan for 15 minutes, then loosen the sides with the dull knife and turn out onto the wire rack. Remove the lining paper and allow to cool completely.
- Cut the cake horizontally into 3 even-sized layers.

⑤
- To make the frosting, put the cream cheese, confectioners' sugar, and orange zest and juice in the second bowl and beat with the wooden spoon until smooth.
- Sandwich the cake layers together with a little of the frosting and spread the rest over the top and sides to completely cover the cake. Transfer to the serving plate.
- Decorate the cake with banana chips and some slices of orange. It is best eaten on the day it is made.

# lemon and cornmeal drizzle cake

cuts into 10 slices

## equipment

pastry brush

2 lb loaf pan (see page 12)

scissors

waxed paper

measuring cups and spoons

large and medium bowls

wooden spoon

fork

grater

toothpick

dessertspoon

lemon squeezer

small saucepan

wire rack

small new paintbrush

4 plates

## ingredients

oil, for greasing

3/4 cup butter, at room temperature

2/3 cup superfine sugar

3 eggs

1 1/2 cups self-rising flour

1/2 cup cornmeal

1 teaspoon baking powder

grated zest of 2 lemons

*Lemon syrup*

juice of 2 lemons

3/4 cup superfine sugar

*To finish (optional)*

1 dried egg white made up with warm water according to package directions

a few fresh primroses, pansies, or violas

superfine sugar, for sprinkling

## what to do

**1** • Set the oven to 350°F.

• Brush the loaf pan with a little oil, then cut a piece of waxed paper to cover the base and the 2 longest sides. Place in the pan and brush lightly with a little extra oil.

**2** • Put the butter and sugar in the large mixing bowl and beat with the wooden spoon until light and fluffy.

- Beat the eggs in the medium bowl with the fork then add alternate spoonfuls of egg and flour to the butter mixture, mixing well until they have all been added. Stir in the cornmeal, baking powder, and lemon zest.

**3**
- Spoon the cake mixture into the pan and smooth flat with the back of the spoon.
- Bake the cake for 40–50 minutes until it is well risen and golden brown, the top is cracked and a toothpick comes out cleanly when pushed into the center of the cake.

**(4)**
- Meanwhile, make the lemon syrup. Put the lemon juice and sugar in the pan and heat gently, stirring until the sugar has dissolved, then boil for 1 minute and set aside.
- Lift the cake out of the pan and put it on the wire rack set over a large plate.
- Make holes with a toothpick in the top of the cake then spoon over the hot lemon syrup so that it runs down into the holes. When all the syrup has been added, leave the cake to cool completely.

**(5)**
- To finish, make up the dried egg white as the package instructs, then brush the liquid over the flowers using the paintbrush.
- Holding one flower at a time over a plate, sprinkle a little sugar over the top using the cleaned dessertspoon. Shake off the excess sugar and put the sugared flowers on the other plate to dry.
- Transfer the cake to the serving plate or board, removing the lining paper. Arrange the sugared flowers on top of the cake just before serving—it is best eaten on the day it is made.

# blueberry and white chocolate cake

cuts into 10 slices

## equipment

pastry brush

2 lb loaf pan (see page 12)

scissors

waxed paper

measuring cups and spoons

plastic bag

rolling pin

large and small bowl

small saucepan

fork

dessertspoon

toothpick

dull knife

wire rack

vegetable peeler

serving plate

## ingredients

oil, for greasing

6 oz white chocolate

2 cups all-purpose flour

2½ teaspoons baking powder

½ cup superfine sugar

¼ cup butter

2 tablespoons sunflower oil

2 tablespoons milk

3 eggs

1 teaspoon vanilla extract

¾ cup fresh blueberries, plus a few extra to decorate

## what to do

**1**
- Set the oven to 350°F.
- Brush the loaf pan with a little oil, then cut a piece of waxed paper to go over the base and up the 2 longest sides. Place in the pan and brush with a little extra oil.
- Put 3½ oz of the white chocolate in the plastic bag and hit with the rolling pin until broken into small chunks.

**2**
- Put the flour, baking powder, and sugar in the large mixing bowl.
- Melt the butter in the pan on the stove. Add the oil, milk, eggs, and vanilla extract and mix together with the fork.
- Pour the butter mixture into the dry ingredients and beat with the fork until only just mixed. Stir in the broken chocolate and the blueberries until just mixed.

**3**
- Spoon the mixture into the pan and smooth flat with the back of the spoon. Bake the cake for 35–45 minutes until it is well risen and golden brown, the top is cracked and a toothpick comes out cleanly when pushed into the center of the cake.
- Leave the cake to cool in the pan for 10 minutes, then loosen the sides with the dull knife and turn out onto the wire rack. Remove the lining paper and allow to cool completely.

**4**
- To finish the cake, break the rest of the white chocolate into pieces and put in the small mixing bowl. Put this over a saucepan of just boiled water and leave for 4–5 minutes until melted.
- Put the cake on the serving plate then spoon melted white chocolate over the top. Add a few blueberries to decorate. Allow to harden before cutting into slices to serve. The cake can be stored in an airtight container for up to 2 days.

# celebration chocolate lace cake

cuts into 8 slices

## equipment

pastry brush

two 8 inch layer cake pans

scissors

waxed paper

kitchen scales, measuring cups, spoons, and jug

small, medium and large mixing bowls

dessertspoon

electric beater or balloon whisk

dull knife

wire rack

saucepan

baking sheet

nonstick parchment paper

cake board

## ingredients

oil, for greasing

½ cup unsweetened cocoa powder

6 tablespoons boiling water

⅔ cup sunflower oil

3 eggs

¾ cup superfine sugar

1½ cups self-rising flour

1½ teaspoons baking powder

*Chocolate lace*

2 oz dark or milk chocolate

2 oz white chocolate

*To finish*

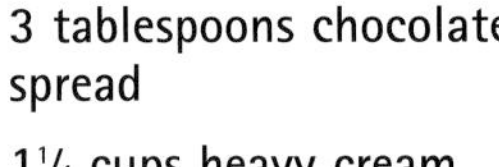

3 tablespoons chocolate spread

1¼ cups heavy cream

## what to do

**1** • Set the oven to 350°F.

• Lightly brush the pans with a little oil, line the bases with circles of waxed paper and brush these with a little extra oil.

• Put the cocoa powder in the small bowl, gradually add the boiling water and mix to a smooth paste with the dessertspoon. Set aside to cool.

2 • Put the oil, eggs, and sugar in the large mixing bowl and beat together. Add the cocoa paste, flour, and baking powder and beat again until smooth.

3 • Divide the mixture between the pans and smooth flat with the back of the spoon.

• Bake the cakes for 18–20 minutes until they are well risen and browned, and the tops spring back when lightly pressed.

• Leave the cakes to cool in the pans for 10 minutes, then loosen the sides with the knife and transfer to the wire rack. Remove the paper and allow to cool completely.

4 • Meanwhile, make the chocolate lace. Break the milk chocolate into pieces and put in the medium bowl set over a pan of boiled water. Leave for 5 minutes until melted.

• Line a baking sheet with nonstick parchment paper then drizzle the melted chocolate over it in wiggly lines. Chill in the refrigerator for 30 minutes until hard.

• Melt the white chocolate in the same way in the washed bowl then drizzle this over the hard chocolate layer and chill again.

5 • Put one of the cakes on the cake board and spread with the chocolate spread.

• Whip the cream in a mixing bowl using the clean whisk until it has just thickened. Spoon half the cream over the chocolate spread. Cover with the second cake then spread the rest of the cream on top.

• Break the chocolate lace into pieces and stand up at angles over the top of the cake. Cut the cake into slices to serve—it is best eaten on the day it is made.

# frosted ginger and date sandwich

cuts into 10 slices

## equipment

pastry brush
8 inch round removable-bottomed pan
scissors
waxed paper
measuring spoons, cups, and jug
medium saucepan
wooden spoon
dessertspoon
3 mixing bowls
fork
toothpick
wire rack and plate
electric beater or balloon whisk
large serrated knife
sifter

## ingredients

oil, for greasing
¼ cup butter
½ cup light corn syrup
⅓ cup light brown sugar
1 cup ready-chopped dates
⅔ cup milk
1 cup self-rising flour
1 cup whole wheat all-purpose or granary flour
2 teaspoons ground ginger
½ teaspoon baking soda
2 eggs

*Banana cream filling*
1 banana
1 tablespoon lemon juice
⅔ cup heavy cream

*To finish*
¾ cup confectioners' sugar
about 3 teaspoons water

## what to do

**1** • Set the oven to 325°F.

• Lightly brush the pan with a little oil, line the base with a circle of waxed paper and brush this lightly with a little extra oil.

**2** • Put the butter, syrup, sugar, dates, and milk in the saucepan and heat gently, stirring with the wooden spoon until the butter has melted and the sugar dissolved.

• Mix the flours, ginger, and baking soda together in one of the bowls.

• Put the eggs in the other bowl and beat with the fork.

**3** • Take the pan off the heat, add the flour mixture and mix until smooth. Add the beaten eggs and beat again until smooth.

**4** • Pour the mixture into the pan. Cook the cake for about 1 hour until it is well risen and deep brown, and a toothpick comes out cleanly when pushed into the center.

• Leave the cake to cool for 10 minutes, then remove the cake from the pan and transfer to the wire rack. Remove the lining paper and allow to cool completely.

**5** • To make the banana cream filling, peel then mash the banana on the plate using the clean fork then mix in the lemon juice.

• Whip the cream in a bowl using the electric beater or balloon whisk until it has just thickened, but be careful not to overwhip or it will look more like butter.

• Stir in the mashed banana.

**(6)** • Cut the cake horizontally into 2 layers using the serrated knife, then sandwich them together with the banana cream.

**(7)** • Sift the confectioners' sugar into one of the cleaned bowls then gradually mix in the water to make a smooth thick icing.

• Drizzle the icing over the top of the cake and leave for 30 minutes to harden. The cake is best eaten on the day it is made.

# raspberry jelly roll

cuts into 8 slices

## ingredients

4 eggs

½ cup superfine sugar, plus a little extra for sprinkling

1 cup all-purpose flour

*To finish*

5 tablespoons raspberry jelly

1¼ cups fresh or frozen raspberries, just thawed

pink and white sugar flowers, to decorate

## equipment

scissors

nonstick parchment paper

medium roasting pan (see page 12)

medium saucepan

measuring cups and spoons

large mixing bowl

electric beater

sifter

large metal spoon

clean dish towel

dull knife

serving plate

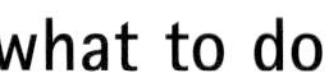

## what to do

**1** • Set the oven to 400°F.

• Cut a piece of nonstick parchment paper a little larger than the pan, snip into the corners and press the paper into the pan.

• Pour water into the saucepan to come about one-third up the sides then heat up.

**(2)** • Put the eggs and sugar in the bowl then set the bowl over the pan of simmering water. Using the electric beater beat the eggs and sugar for 5 minutes until very thick and foamy. To check whether it is thick enough, lift the beaters and drizzle a little mixture over the top of the bowl. If the trail stays for a few seconds it is ready.

• Sift the flour over the top, gently fold it into the beaten eggs and sugar with the spoon.

2

4

**3** • Pour the cake mixture into the pan and ease it into the corners by tipping the pan slightly and very gently using the spoon.

• Bake the cake for 8–10 minutes until it is golden brown and just beginning to shrink away from the paper, and the top spring backs when lightly pressed.

• Meanwhile, wet the dish towel with warm water then wring it out. Put the dish towel on the countertop with one of the short sides facing you.

• Cover the dish towel with a piece of nonstick parchment paper then sprinkle lightly with a little sugar.

**4** • Tip the cake and the lining paper onto the paper-topped dish towel. Peel away the lining paper and then, working quickly, spread the cake with the jelly. Sprinkle with two-thirds of the raspberries.

• Using the paper under the cake and the dish towel to help, roll up the cake from the shortest edge nearest you, gradually peeling away the paper and cloth as you work toward the opposite short edge.

• Wrap the paper tightly around the cake and leave for 1–2 minutes to set the rolled-up shape.

• Transfer the cake to the serving plate and decorate with the remaining raspberries and a few sugar flowers. Cut the cake into thick slices to serve—it is best eaten on the day it is made.

# creamy kiwi meringue gâteau

cuts into 8 slices

## equipment

2 baking sheets
scissors
nonstick parchment paper
pencil
large and medium mixing bowls
electric beater
measuring cups, spoons, and jug
teaspoon
cup
dessertspoon
vegetable peeler
small sharp knife
cutting board
serving plate

## ingredients

4 egg whites
½ cup superfine sugar
½ cup light brown sugar
1 teaspoon cornstarch
1 teaspoon white wine vinegar

*To finish*
4 kiwi fruit
¾ cup seedless grapes
1¼ cups heavy cream

## what to do

**1** • Set the oven to 225°F.

• Line the baking sheets with pieces of nonstick parchment paper and draw a 9 inch circle on one and a 7 inch circle on the other, using cake pans as templates to draw around.

**2** • Put the egg whites in the large bowl and beat using the electric beater until very stiff. To test whether they are ready, turn the bowl upside down—if the eggs look like they may slide out, beat for a few minutes more.

3

5

- Gradually beat in the sugars, a teaspoonful at a time, and continue beating for 1–2 minutes more, even when all the sugar has been added, so that the meringue is very thick and glossy.
- Mix the cornstarch and vinegar in the cup then beat into the meringue.

**3**
- Spoon the meringue onto the lined baking sheets and spread within the marked circles.
- Bake the meringue layers for 1¼ hours or until they can be lifted easily off the paper.
- Allow to cool on the paper. Don't worry if the meringues crack slightly.

**4**
- To finish the gâteau, peel the brown skin away from the kiwi fruit and discard, then cut the fruit into slices.
- Cut the grapes in half.
- Whip the cream in the second bowl using the cleaned beaters until the cream has thickened and makes soft swirls.

**5**
- Lift the larger meringue off its lining paper and put on the serving plate. Spread with the cream and arrange the fruit on top.
- Add the other meringue layer and store in the refrigerator until needed—it is best eaten on the day it is made.

# baked strawberry and lime cheesecake

cuts into 8 slices

## equipment

scissors

nonstick parchment paper

8 inch round springform pan

small serrated knife

cutting board

grater

lemon squeezer

kitchen scale and measuring cups and spoons

large and medium mixing bowls

2 cups or small bowls

electric beater

dessertspoon

serving plate

## ingredients

4 sponge cakes

1 lime

13 oz full-fat cream cheese

½ cup superfine sugar

2 tablespoons all-purpose flour

4 eggs

*To finish*

½ cup full-fat crème fraîche or sour cream

1⅔ cups hulled strawberries

## what to do

1
- Set the oven to 325°F.
- Line the base and sides of the pan with nonstick parchment paper (see page 12).
- Cut the sponge cakes in half horizontally and then into triangles. Arrange them over the base of the pan so that it is completely covered.

2
- Finely grate the zest from the lime then cut in half and squeeze the juice.

1

2

- Put the cream cheese, sugar, and flour in the large mixing bowl.
- Separate the eggs, adding the yolks to the cream cheese mixture and putting the whites in the medium mixing bowl.
- Beat the egg whites using the electric beater until they are thick.
- Using the still dirty beater beat the cream cheese mixture until smooth then beat in the lime zest and juice.
- Gently fold the egg whites into the cream cheese mixture using the metal spoon until evenly mixed.

**3**
- Pour the mixture into the sponge-lined pan and bake the cheesecake for 50–60 minutes until it is pale golden brown and the center still wobbles slightly.
- Turn the oven off, open the door slightly and leave the cheesecake in the oven for 15 minutes.
- Take the cheesecake out of the oven and allow to cool completely.

**4**
- Remove the pan and lining paper from the cheesecake and put it on the plate. Spoon the crème fraîche or sour cream on top and smooth with the back of the spoon. Decorate with the strawberries and chill until ready to serve.

# farmhouse white loaf

## ingredients

- oil, for greasing
- 4 cups bread flour, plus a little extra for dusting the countertop
- ½ teaspoon salt
- 2 teaspoons superfine sugar
- 1 package or 2 teaspoons active dry yeast
- 2 tablespoons sunflower oil
- 1–1¼ cups warm water

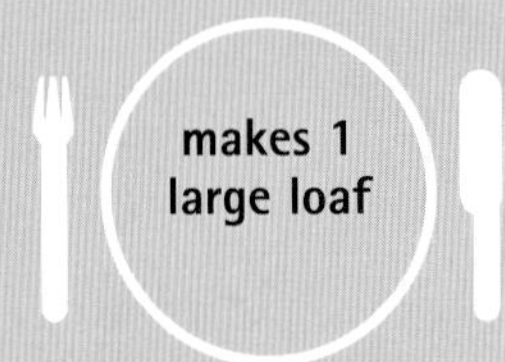


## equipment

- pastry brush
- 2 lb loaf pan (see page 12)
- measuring cups, spoons, and jug
- large mixing bowl
- wooden spoon
- plastic wrap
- dull knife
- wire rack

## what to do

**1** • Lightly brush the loaf pan with a little oil.

**(2)** • Put the flour, salt, sugar, and yeast in the mixing bowl.

• Add the oil then gradually mix in just enough of the warm water to mix to a soft but not sticky dough, using the wooden spoon at first then later squeezing together with your hands.

• Sprinkle the countertop with a little flour then knead the dough for 5 minutes until it is smooth and elastic.

**(3)** • Shape the dough into a sausage shape about the length of the loaf pan with your hands then lift up and press into the oiled pan.

- Cover the top of the dough loosely with lightly greased plastic wrap then leave in a warm place for 30–45 minutes until it has risen just above the top of the pan. Toward the end of the rising time set the oven to 400°F to allow it to warm up before using.

**4**
- Remove the plastic wrap and sprinkle the dough with a little flour.
- Bake the bread for 25–30 minutes until it is well risen and golden brown.
- Loosen the sides with the dull knife then turn out and allow to cool on the wire rack. The bread can be stored in a bread bin for up to 2 days.

## tip

★ When it is cooked, the base of the loaf should sound hollow when tapped with your fingertips. If the bread feels a little soft on the base after you have turned it out, put it back in the oven without the pan, straight onto the oven shelf, and bake it for 5 more minutes.

# soft seeded granary rolls

makes 16

## equipment

pastry brush

large baking sheet

measuring cups, spoons, and jug

large mixing bowl

wooden spoon

dull knife

plastic wrap

## ingredients

oil, for greasing

3¼ cups granary or whole wheat all-purpose flour, plus a little extra for dusting the countertop

¼ teaspoon salt

1½ teaspoons active dry yeast

3 teaspoons honey

1 tablespoon olive or sunflower oil

¾–1 cup warm water

*topping*

1 egg yolk

a few sunflower, poppy, and sesame seeds

## what to do

**1**
- Lightly brush the baking sheet with oil.

**2**
- Put the flour, salt, and yeast in the bowl.
- Add the honey and oil then gradually mix in just enough of the warm water to mix to a soft but not sticky dough, using the wooden spoon at first then later squeezing together with your hands.

**(3)**
- Sprinkle the countertop with a little flour then knead the dough for 5 minutes until it is smooth and elastic.
- Cut the dough into quarters, then cut each quarter into 4 more pieces. Shape each piece into a round ball with your hands.

3

4

- Place the balls in rows of 4 on the oiled baking sheet, leaving a little space in between each ball to allow the rolls to rise and spread.
- Cover loosely with lightly greased plastic wrap then allow to rise in a warm place for 30–40 minutes until the rolls are half as big again. Toward the end of the rising time set the oven to 400°F to allow it to warm up before using it to cook the bread.

(4)

- Remove the plastic wrap and brush the rolls gently with the egg yolk. Sprinkle each row of rolls with a different kind of seed.
- Bake the rolls for 8–10 minutes until they are well risen and browned, and the bases sound hollow when tapped with fingertips.
- Leave the rolls to cool on the baking sheet. Serve them warm or cold with butter—they are best eaten on the day they are made.

# herb and sun-dried tomato bread

cuts into 10 slices

## equipment

pastry brush

8 inch loose-bottomed or springform pan

scissors

kitchen scale, measuring cups, spoons, and jug

large mixing bowl

wooden spoon

plastic wrap

dull knife

wire rack

## ingredients

oil, for greasing

small bunch of fresh chives

3 or 4 sprigs of fresh rosemary, plus a little extra for sprinkling

3 oz drained sun-dried tomatoes in oil

1¾ cups bread flour, plus a little extra for dusting the countertop

1¾ cups granary or whole wheat all-purpose flour, plus a little extra for sprinkling

¼ teaspoon salt

1 teaspoon superfine sugar

1½ teaspoons active dry yeast

2 tablespoons olive oil or oil from the sun-dried tomatoes jar

¾–1 cup warm water

## what to do

1 • Lightly brush the cake pan with a little oil.

• Snip the chives into pieces with the scissors to fill about 3 tablespoons and the rosemary to fill about 1 tablespoon then snip the sun-dried tomatoes into pieces.

2 • Put the flours, salt, sugar, and yeast in the mixing bowl.

• Add the herbs and tomatoes and the oil then mix in just enough warm water to

1

3

make a soft but not sticky dough, using the wooden spoon at first then later squeezing together with your hands.

3 • Sprinkle the countertop with a little flour then knead the dough for 5 minutes until it is smooth and elastic.

• Shape into a ball then press into the base of the pan. Cover loosely with lightly oiled plastic wrap then leave in a warm place for 30–40 minutes until the dough is half as big again or near the top of the pan. Toward the end of the rising time set the oven to 400°F to allow it to warm up before using.

**4** • Remove the plastic wrap and sprinkle the dough with a few extra snipped rosemary leaves and some extra granary flour.

• Bake the bread for 20–25 minutes until it is deep brown and the base sounds hollow when tapped with fingertips.

• Loosen the edge of the bread with the dull knife. Release from the pan and tip out onto the wire rack. Allow to cool, then slice the bread and serve with cheese or soup.

## tip

★ Instead of making a loaf you could cut the dough into 12 pieces and shape them into rolls. Leave the rolls to rise for 30 minutes then sprinkle with flour and cook for 10 minutes.

# basil, garlic, and cheese twist

makes 2 loaves; each cuts into 8 pieces

## equipment

pastry brush

large baking sheet

kitchen scale, measuring cups, spoons, and jug

large mixing bowl

wooden spoon

rolling pin

dull knife

garlic press

grater

plastic wrap

spatula

wire rack

## ingredients

oil, for greasing

$3\frac{1}{4}$ cups bread flour, plus a little extra for dusting the countertop

$\frac{1}{4}$ teaspoon salt

1 teaspoon superfine sugar

$1\frac{1}{2}$ teaspoons active dry yeast

2 tablespoons sunflower oil

$\frac{3}{4}$–1 cup warm water

*To finish*

$\frac{1}{4}$ cup butter, at room temperature

3 garlic cloves

small bunch of fresh basil

4 oz cheddar cheese

## what to do

**1** • Lightly brush the baking sheet with oil.

**2** • Put the flour, salt, sugar, and yeast in the mixing bowl and stir together.

• Add the oil then mix in just enough warm water to make a soft but not sticky dough, using the wooden spoon at first then later squeezing together with your hands.

• Sprinkle the countertop with a little flour then knead the dough for 5 minutes until it is smooth and elastic.

3 • Roll the dough out thinly to make a rectangle about 10 x 18 inches.

• Spread the dough with the butter. Crush the garlic, tear the basil leaves from the stems, keeping a few back for the top of the dough, and sprinkle the garlic and basil over the butter.

• Grate the cheese then sprinkle over the dough, keeping a little back for the top of the dough.

4 • Roll up the dough from one of the longest edges over to the other.

• Twist the dough several times then cut in half to make 2 long loaves.

5 • Put the loaves on the oiled baking sheet, leaving a little space in between them. Sprinkle with the reserved basil leaves and cheese.

• Cover loosely with lightly oiled plastic wrap then leave in a warm place for 30 minutes to rise. Toward the end of the rising time set the oven to 400°F to allow it to warm up before using.

• Remove the plastic wrap and bake the loaves for 15 minutes until golden brown and the bases sound hollow when tapped with fingertips.

• Loosen the bread with the spatula then transfer to the wire rack. Serve the bread warm or cold, thickly sliced, with barbecued meats and salad or with bowls of soup. It is best eaten on the day it is made.

# sausage pizza squares

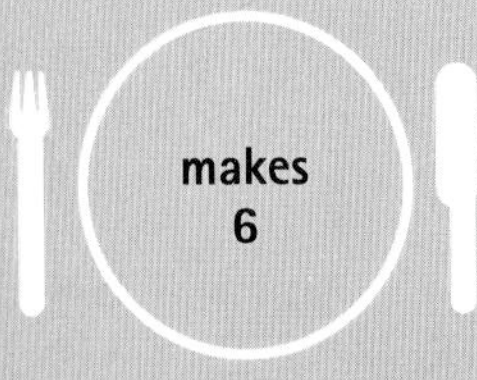


## equipment

pastry brush

2 large baking sheets

kitchen scale, measuring cups, spoons, and jug

large mixing bowl

wooden spoon

rolling pin

small sharp knife

dull knife

cutting board

grater

## ingredients

oil, for greasing

3¼ cups bread flour, plus a little extra for dusting the countertop

¼ teaspoon salt

1 teaspoon superfine sugar

1½ teaspoons active dry yeast

2 tablespoons olive oil

¾–1 cup warm water

*Pizza topping*

4 tablespoons tomato sauce (ketchup)

3 fresh tomatoes

small bunch of fresh basil

4 cooked sausages

4 chilled frankfurters

3 oz cheddar cheese

## what to do

**1** • Lightly brush the baking sheets with a little oil.

**2** • Put the flour, salt, sugar, and yeast in the large mixing bowl.

• Add the oil then gradually mix in just enough of the warm water to mix to a soft but not sticky dough, using the wooden spoon at first then later squeezing together with your hands.

3 • Sprinkle the countertop with a little flour then knead the dough for 5 minutes until it is smooth and elastic.

• Roll the dough out very thinly to a roughly shaped rectangle, about 15 x 10 inches, then cut into 6 smaller equal-sized squares.

• Transfer the squares to the baking sheets, leaving a little space in between to allow the dough to rise and spread.

④ • Spread the top of the pizzas with the tomato sauce, leaving a border of dough still showing.

• Cut the tomatoes into small pieces on the cutting board, arrange on top of the tomato sauce then tear the basil into pieces and sprinkle on the top.

• Thinly slice the cooked sausages and thickly slice the frankfurters. Arrange on top of the tomatoes then grate the cheese and sprinkle on top.

• Leave the pizzas in a warm place to rise (uncovered) for 30 minutes. Toward the end of the rising time set the oven to 425°F to allow it to warm up before using.

5 • Bake the pizzas for 10–12 minutes until the cheese is bubbling. Serve the pizzas warm with cucumber and carrot sticks—they are best eaten on the day they are made.

# raisin soda bread

makes 1 round loaf; cuts into 8 thick slices

## equipment

pastry brush

baking sheet

measuring cups, spoons, and jug

large mixing bowl

wooden spoon

small saucepan or microwave-proof bowl

rolling pin

sharp knife

clean dish towel or wire rack

## ingredients

oil, for greasing

1⅓ cups granary or whole wheat all-purpose flour

1½ cups all-purpose flour, plus a little extra for dusting the countertop

pinch of salt

2 teaspoons cream of tartar

1 teaspoon baking soda

¼ cup light brown sugar

¾ cup golden raisins

2 tablespoons butter

about ¾ cup warm milk

## what to do

**1**
- Set the oven to 400°F.
- Lightly brush the baking sheet with oil.

**2**
- Put the flours, salt, cream of tartar, baking soda, sugar, and golden raisins in the mixing bowl and mix together.

**(3)**
- Melt the butter in the saucepan on the stove, or in the bowl in the microwave on full power for 30 seconds.
- Add the melted butter to the flour mixture then gradually mix in just enough of the warm milk to mix to a soft and slightly sticky dough.

(3)

(4)

4
- Sprinkle the countertop with a little flour then knead the dough for 1 minute until it is just smooth.
- Roll out the dough to make a thick 6 inch circle.
- Put on the oiled baking sheet and score a cross right over the top.
- Sprinkle with a little all-purpose flour then bake the bread for about 25 minutes until it is well risen and browned, and the base sounds hollow when tapped.

5
- Wrap in the clean dish towel and allow to cool for a soft crust or, for a crisp crust, leave the loaf to cool unwrapped on the wire rack. Serve the bread warm or cold, thickly sliced and spread with butter. It is best eaten on the day it is made, although any leftovers can be toasted on the following day.

## tip

★ Mixed dried fruit, chopped dried apricots, peaches or dates could also be added in place of the golden raisins.

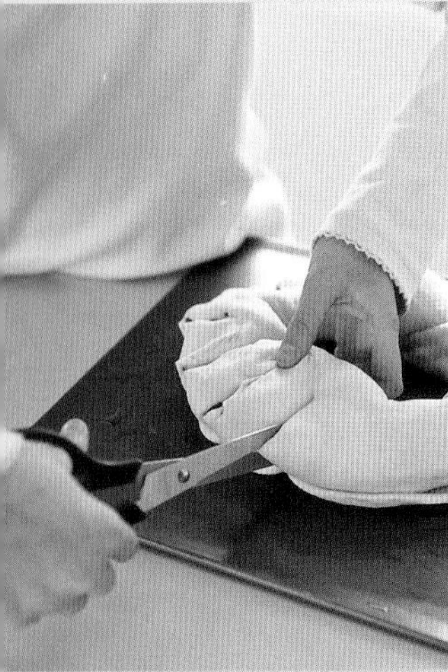

# fruited tea ring

serves 8

## equipment

pastry brush
large baking sheet
measuring cups, spoons, and jug
large and small bowls
wooden spoon
rolling pin
dull knife
grater
small sharp knife
scissors
plastic wrap
wire rack
sifter
lemon squeezer
dessertspoon
serving plate

## ingredients

oil, for greasing

3¼ cups bread flour, plus a little extra for dusting the countertop

¼ teaspoon salt

1 tablespoon light brown sugar

1½ teaspoons active dry yeast

2 tablespoons sunflower oil

¾–1 cup warm water

*To finish*

¼ cup butter, at room temperature

4 tablespoons light brown sugar

grated zest and juice of ½ orange

⅓ cup candied cherries, plus a few extra for decorating

½ cup ready-to-eat dried apricots, plus a few extra for decorating

½ cup mixed dried fruit or golden raisins

milk, for glazing

1 cup confectioners' sugar

a few strips of candied angelica, to decorate

## what to do

**1** • Lightly brush the baking sheet with oil.

**2** • Put the flour, salt, sugar, and yeast in the large mixing bowl.

• Add the oil then mix in just enough of the warm water to make a soft but not sticky dough, using the wooden spoon at first then squeezing together with your hands.

5

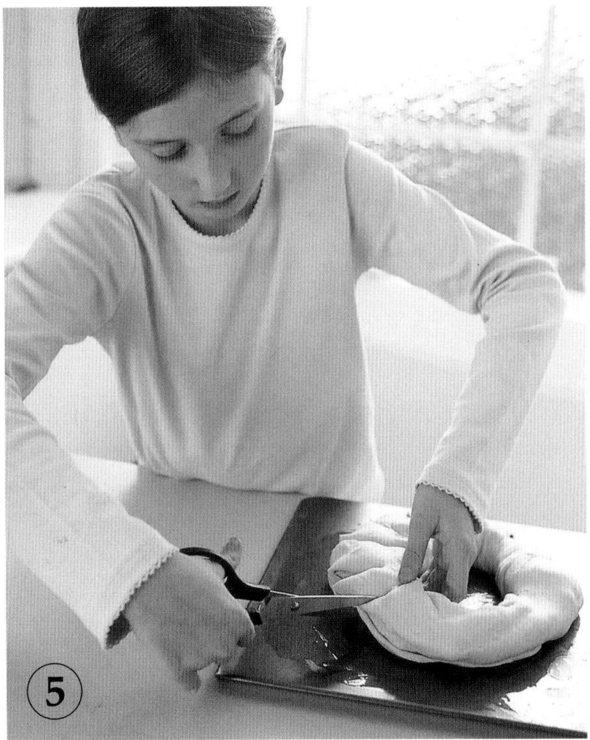

5

**3** • Sprinkle the countertop with a little flour then knead the dough for 5 minutes until it is smooth and elastic.

• Roll out the dough thinly to make a large rectangle, 10 x 18 inches.

**4** • Spread the dough with the butter then sprinkle with the sugar and orange zest.

• Cut the cherries into small pieces. Snip the apricots into small pieces with the scissors. Sprinkle the cherries, apricots, and mixed dried fruit over the dough.

**(5)** • Starting from one of the longest edges, roll up the dough. Stick the edges together with a little milk brushed on.

• Lift the dough onto the baking sheet and shape into a large ring, squeezing the ends together and sticking in place with milk.

• Using the scissors, make 8 small cuts in the dough at intervals around the outside edge.

• Cover loosely with greased plastic wrap then allow to rise in a warm place for 30–40 minutes until the dough is half as big again. Near the end of the rising time set the oven to 400°F.

**6** • Remove the plastic wrap, brush the dough with a little milk and bake the bread ring for 15 minutes until it is golden brown and the base sounds hollow when tapped. Carefully transfer to the wire rack to cool.

• To make the icing, sift the confectioners' sugar into the small bowl then gradually mix in the orange juice to make a smooth icing.

• Put the ring on the serving plate, spoon the icing over the top then decorate with the extra pieces of cherry and dried apricot to look like flowers and use the angelica for the flower "stems." Leave for 30 minutes then cut the ring into thick slices—it is best eaten on the day it is made.

# sticky glazed orange starbursts

makes 20

## equipment

measuring cups, spoons, and jug

mortar and pestle or mug and rolling pin

small saucepan

pastry brush

2 large baking sheets

plastic wrap

large mixing bowl

grater

wooden spoon

dull knife

scissors

lemon squeezer

wire rack

## ingredients

2 teaspoons coriander seeds

2 tablespoons butter

4 cups bread flour, plus a little extra for dusting the countertop

1 teaspoon superfine sugar

1 teaspoon salt

grated zest of 1 orange

1½ teaspoons active dry yeast

1–1¼ cups warm water

*To finish*

juice of ½ orange

2 tablespoons honey

crushed sugar cubes and grated orange zest, to decorate (optional)

## what to do

1 • Crush the coriander seeds using a mortar and pestle or by putting the seeds in the mug and grinding them with the end of the rolling pin.

• Melt the butter in the pan on the stove. Use a little butter to brush over the baking sheets and 2 large sheets of plastic wrap.

2 • Put half the coriander seeds in the bowl. Add the flour, sugar, salt, orange zest, and yeast and mix together.

1

3

- Pour the remaining butter into the flour mixture. Gradually mix in enough of the warm water to mix to a soft but not sticky dough, using the wooden spoon at first and later squeezing together in your hands.

**3**
- Sprinkle the countertop with a little flour then knead the dough for 5 minutes until it is smooth and elastic.
- Cut into 20 pieces then shape each piece into a ball.
- Using the scissors, make 5 cuts around the edge of each ball, but not right into the center. Transfer the balls to the baking sheets, leaving a little space in between to allow the rolls to rise and spread.

**4**
- Sprinkle the rolls with the rest of the coriander seeds. Cover loosely with the buttered plastic wrap and leave to rise in a warm place for 30–40 minutes until the rolls are half as big again. Near the end of the rising time set the oven to 400°F to allow it to warm up.

**5**
- Remove the plastic wrap and bake the rolls for 10 minutes until golden brown and the bases sound hollow when tapped.
- Meanwhile, make an orange glaze by warming the orange juice and honey together in the cleaned pan until melted.
- Transfer the hot rolls to the wire rack and brush with the honey mixture. Sprinkle them with the crushed sugar cubes and extra grated orange zest, if you like—they are best eaten on the day they are made.

# deep-pan fruit salad pizza

## equipment

pastry brush

11 inch removable-bottomed tart pan

measuring cups, spoons, and jug

large and medium mixing bowls

small saucepan or microwave-proof bowl

wooden spoon

dessertspoon

vegetable peeler

small sharp knife

cutting board

lemon squeezer

kitchen foil

sifter

## ingredients

oil, for greasing

2½ cups bread flour, plus a little extra for dusting the countertop

pinch of salt

2 tablespoons superfine sugar

1½ teaspoons active dry yeast

2 tablespoons butter

1 egg

about ½ cup warm water

*Topping*

4 tablespoons strawberry jelly

2 dessert apples

2 tablespoons lemon juice

2 ripe plums

3 small peaches

2 tablespoons butter

2 tablespoons superfine sugar

sifted confectioners' sugar, for dusting

## what to do

**1** • Lightly brush the tart pan with a little oil.

**2** • Put the flour, salt, sugar, and yeast in the large bowl.

• Melt the butter in the saucepan on the stove, or in the medium bowl in the microwave on full power for 30 seconds.

- Add the butter and the egg to the flour mixture then slowly mix in just enough warm water to make a soft but not sticky dough. Use the wooden spoon at first then squeeze the dough with your hands.

**3**
- Sprinkle the countertop with a little flour then knead the dough for 5 minutes until it is smooth and elastic.
- Put the dough in the pan and press over the base with your hands. Spoon on the jelly.

**4**
- Quarter, core, and peel the apples, then cut each piece in half again. Put in the cleaned medium bowl and toss in the lemon juice.
- Cut the plums and peaches into halves. Cut away the pits. Thickly slice the fruit and arrange the 3 different fruits in rings on top of the pizza dough.
- Leave in a warm place for the dough to rise (uncovered) for 30–40 minutes. Toward the end of the rising time set the oven to 400°F to allow it to warm up before using.

**5**
- Melt the butter as before, brush over the fruit and sprinkle with the superfine sugar.
- Bake the pizza for 15 minutes then reduce the oven temperature to 350°F and cook for 20–30 minutes more until the base is cooked. Check the pizza and cover with foil if it is browning too quickly.

**6**
- When cooked, dust the pizza with confectioners' sugar and remove it from the hot pan. Cut it into wedges and serve warm or cold—it is best eaten on the day it is made.

# index

# acknowledgments

**Photography** © Octopus Publishing Group Ltd/Vanessa Davies
**Food Styling** Sara Lewis
**Executive Editor** Nicky Hill
**Editor** Jessica Cowie
**Executive Art Editor** Rozelle Bentheim
**Designer** One 2 Six Creative
**Senior Production Controller** Manjit Sihra